UNOFFENDABLE

NO OFFENSE. NONE TAKEN.

WRITTEN BY RYAN LEAK

EDITED BY AMY NOELCK
DESIGNED BY JASEN ROMAN

NAVIGATION

THE PRE-FOREWORD

I know this is the part of the book where I'm supposed to reach out to someone famous and have him or her endorse everything that you are about to read. But being honest, all the famous people I know would have no idea if what I write down on paper would be something I would actually live out in my daily life. So I'd rather you hear from someone who is famous in my book and knows me beyond social media highlights.

Here's what you need to know about him:

He's a husband, pastor, speaker, writer, and most likely, a soon-to-be father. (I'm praying for triplets.)

He's known for his extreme kindness and generosity toward others. But most importantly, he's the most authentic and loyal friend I have ever known. Ladies and gentlemen, give it up for James Wilson.

FOREWORD

Ryan asked me to write the foreword to his book because in his words, "You actually know me. I could try and get someone more well-known to do it, but they'll have to make up a bunch of stuff to try and sound like we are close. I want someone to write it who can speak to the person I am. *Someone with beautiful prose who has mastered the power of linguistics. Someone who is both the voice of the common and the aristocratic man. In short... I need you James.*"

Some of that quote was actually said.

When Ryan sent me the first draft of this book to look over, he warned me I would show up in a story about halfway through. Very flattered, I asked what the story was. He said it was the story of the last time I evaluated a project of his, and how my scathing review of it offended him deeply...then he asked me to critique this book and write the foreword.

I didn't feel awkward though. Why? Because Ryan not only practices what he preaches, he practices what he writes, advises, tweets, and posts. When Ryan writes a book called *UnOffendable*, it's because Ryan gets offended, but Ryan doesn't stay offended.

The Bible has this profound verse where it tells Christians to make allowance for each other's faults. In a world full of offended people offending people, I've never known anyone to be better at making allowance for other people's offensive behavior than Ryan Leak. He forgives. He moves on. This doesn't simply make Ryan a great friend to have, but it makes him an easy friend to keep. His inability to stay offended makes him a skillful friend and a loyal one too. In short, Ryan makes friendship easy.

When I read *Unoffendable*, I did not run across a single suggestion or principle I had not personally watched Ryan live out in person. In fact, I felt like I had already read the book, because I have been fortunate enough to have experienced, first hand, what these principals can do in someone's life through having a front row seat to watching Ryan learn and live this out for over a decade now.

What I want you to know is this: the book you're reading was *not* written by a guy who is low on character, high on free time, or equipped with a word processor. It was written by a great friend who enjoys nothing more than helping other people live in complete freedom.

There is a better life ahead of you. A life where words sting, but don't stick. A life where what has been done to you does not define you. A life where you can receive criticism and not be crippled by it. Finally, I hope you find in these pages what God wants for you, and what Ryan wants for you: freedom.

Ryan also said I could write the foreword because, "Nobody reads it anyway." Cheers to you if you did.

- James Wilson

LET'S BEGIN

Sticks and stones may break my bones, but words will never hurt me.

How awesome would it be if that statement were true? Oftentimes it is much easier to heal a broken bone than it is to heal the wound caused by something someone said that deeply offended us.

One of the greatest threats to our happiness is holding on to an offense. One offense has the ability to ruin someone's day, someone's week, someone's month, someone's year, or for some... their entire life.

Sometimes the worst part of an offense isn't **what** was said, but **who** said it. The pain of an offense often hinges on the person behind the discouragement. Whether the offenses come from a family member, boss, pastor, teacher, coach, friend, colleague, or lover—their words have the ability to destroy every dream you have, especially when it's someone who carries authority over you. There is no pain quite like the kind you receive from someone you look up to.

Other times, being offended has nothing to do with who said it at all. Instead, the pain of the offense is coming directly from the core of an already established insecurity. Maybe someone made a negative comment about how you look and the statement itself hurt so deeply that it continues to have the ability to make you obsess over your appearance.

My father was 49 years old when I was born. So by the time I was playing basketball in high school, my dad was already in his 60s. Complete strangers would often ask me if the man cheering insanely loud for me in the bleachers was my *grandfather*. To this day, I no longer remember their names or their faces, but what I do remember clearly is the feeling of being emotionally paralyzed and honestly... *offended*.

Regardless of our age, wealth, career, relationship status, or spiritual maturity, no one is exempt from offenses. Part of our human nature lies in wanting other humans to think highly of us. We want to be desired by the opposite sex. We want people to think we are good looking, wealthy, and ultimately happy. We want people to think we have it all together, living in a constant state of success.

When we hear criticism and negative opinions, our self-esteem is attacked. It's one thing for you to feel successful, but it helps if other people agree.

Ultimately, it's our desire for other people to agree with the highest opinion we have of ourselves. We want other people to agree with what we continually *tell ourselves* about ourselves. You can tell yourself you are a great dad, but no matter how confident you are in parenting, your child's opinion plays a major role in becoming a great parent. You can see yourself as a beautiful person, but until you hear a compliment congruent with that thought, you may not really believe it at your core.

We have all had a moment where somebody said something that made us feel unappreciated, insignificant, and undervalued.

Maybe it was a racial slur.

Maybe it was a sexist remark.

Maybe it was a Facebook comment.

Maybe it was a breakup and seeing him or her with somebody else makes you calculate everything wrong with you and right with whomever they chose.

Maybe it was a heated conversation with your spouse and lines were crossed that made you feel as if your relationship may never be repaired.

Sometimes we're offended not because of something someone said or did to us, but because of something someone said or did to a *person we love*. Under the umbrella of being a good friend, we'll become offended on behalf of other people.

Sometimes an offense comes, not from what a person has actually said, but from what they *never said* that you longed to hear. When you hear other people being complimented for the exact same thing you work your butt off to do, it's easy for your passion to diminish.

This happens when a father is proud of one kid and not the other. It's one thing to receive love because we're related. It's another thing to receive love because the person legitimately loves who we are and what we do. You'd be shocked to hear the amount of money a person would be willing to spend to hear their dad simply say he was genuinely proud of them.

Perhaps, the company's decision to hire someone else made you question your own abilities. Maybe an investor liked your idea, but not enough to write you a check. You're confident in the work you do, but in your mind you will never be as good as _____ in the minds of other people.

An offense can come from anywhere and anyone, and the closer the words come to devaluing what we treasure most about ourselves, the stronger the sting.

What if I told you that you could live a life where you were unoffendable?

Not invincible.
Not Superman.
Not Wonder Woman.

No, you'll certainly bleed. But what if I told you your pain could have a purpose? What if you could hear an offense and actually know what to do with it? What if I could tell you when offenses would come and that you could actually prepare yourself to handle them before they reached your heart?

Can you imagine if and when someone else was chosen over you, it no longer diminished your own identity, but instead, brought clarity to your destiny?

The Bible clearly tells us there are spiritual weapons designed to destroy our hopes and dreams. That's life. Those weapons often come in the form of offenses. The good news, however, is those weapons don't have to prosper. Offenses, criticisms, and negative opinions can and will come your way, but the Bible shows us how to handle these situations in a Godly way.

UnOffendable is an outline of how God can use the things in life that have hurt us the most, to shape our confidence and help us become the people we've always wanted to be. You can get offended, but you don't have to *stay* offended.

Let's begin.

1

THE CRITIC IN ME

If you were able to sit in my mother's living room and look through photo albums from my childhood, you'd be shocked to see I pretty much look exactly the same. I've undoubtedly added a small amount of facial hair, but I have received the same type of haircut since I was 5 years old. Sadly, even the size and shape of my head has not changed since I was an adolescent. The only difference, now in my 30s, is my body finally caught up with my head. So you can imagine, the one thing I was made fun of the most for in middle school was the abnormal largeness of my immense dome.

My peers got pretty creative with the nicknames assigned to me and would discover objects around the classroom that were similar to the shape of my head for comparison. One girl regularly noted I had 4 distinct corners on my head and would call me, "Four Corners." During one lunch hour, the top of my head was referred to as a baseball diamond. If she went to the right side of my head, one could say she went to "first base" with Ryan. (Middle school is brutal.)

Before you start feeling sorry for me, I was just fine. I picked up a bad habit of defending myself. I believed the cure for an offense was *defense*. So I decided if others had something negative to say about me, I just had to have better jokes and comebacks. If I happened to be put down, I would come up with something to say that would bring my opponent down further.

I wasn't mean.

I was *meaner*.

But what all of this got me, and what it got the person who called me, "friend", was *nothing*. We only became two mean people who didn't speak to each other when we passed in the hallway.

To this day, I can remember most of the nicknames and smart remarks my peers made about me in our adolescence. Yet for some reason, I no longer remember any of my comebacks. What I remember more than anything, are the results of my defenses through my comebacks and the affect they had on the lives of those on the receiving end.

What I know about us, as the human race, is this: the moments we have been offended by someone else are always crystal clear. Yet the moments we have been the cause of an offense for another remain quite blurry. Ironically, though we all grow up eventually, a part of us is still at the middle school lunch table when it comes to how we choose to deal with offenses.

We learn defense mechanisms as teenagers that can take over, without warning, when we become adults. One of the most underrated defense mechanisms we have is our ability to criticize other people.

Most of us seldom do this out loud, but

privately, merely diminishing someone else's success makes us feel better about our own shortcomings. It's as though another person's things, careers, and relationships are in direct competition with our things, our careers, and our relationships. But as long as we see our friends and their lives as secret competition, we will always incidentally offend other people because we find it so stinking hard to just be happy for them. It's amazing how people can spend an hour on social media and internally criticize what everyone else is posting.

It's not always easy to be happy for all of your friends who are getting engaged when you're still single.

It's difficult to be happy for your friends who keep getting raises when you are unable to find work.

It's harder still to be excited for someone who received the promotion you believe you deserved.

These situations can make you feel as if someone else's winning is somehow a direct result of your losing. Comparison has a way of making you feel as if another person's success equals your failure.

Giving in to these negative feelings will lead you to mere *golf-clapping* for another person's achievements, rather than genuinely celebrating them. If these feelings are not managed, you will consistently find flaws in other people, yet become offended when anyone points out a flaw in you.

To build a solid framework for living an unoffendable life, you have to remember this: **You will reap what you sow**. Life is not about what you receive. Life is all about what you *give*.

I decided, a long time ago, I want to be known as a cheerleader for my family, friends, and the people I love the most. The life of a fan is so much more enjoyable than the life of a hater. When I began intentionally celebrating other people, I actually found myself becoming *less* offended and less offending.

Genuine celebration of another person's success disarms the trap of comparison.

OFFENSE BY COMPARISON

As a speaker, author, and filmmaker, I'm tempted to compare my messages, books, and films to other communicators, writers, and artists. But my goal isn't to become the best speaker, author, and filmmaker *in the world*. My goal is to become the best speaker, author, and filmmaker *I can* be.

I don't need to be a better speaker than _____ to feel like I'm a legit communicator.

I don't need to write better than _____ to feel like I'm a distinguished author.

I don't need to create films better than _____ to feel like I'm an accomplished storyteller.

I'm not trying to be *the* best, but simply trying to give *my* best.

God will never ask you to be better than someone else, He will only ask you to give the best of everything *you have* to Him.

Accepting this truth was freeing for me

because it made me capable of genuinely celebrating other talented speakers, authors, and filmmakers without diminishing my own gifts and talents. Not only do I celebrate who they are, but now I can actually learn from others without critiquing them in my head.

THE GOAL OF CHATTER

Another part of being unoffendable is simply being less offensive to others. There are a lot of people who have offended you and they don't even know they have.

On the other hand, you have offended other people and they simply have yet to tell you.

I've had several friends over the years who are unsure of how to talk to me or others about racial issues existing in our country for the fear they may *sound* offensive. However, I believe the best thing we can do in conversations like these is to ask genuine questions in love.

Asking questions can create healthy dialogue around tense topics. This gives you the opportunity to understand other people's perspective and narrows the gap for offense to govern your conversations. I love how Paul talked about this in Colossians:

> "The goal is to **bring out the best** in the others in a conversation, not put them down, not cut them out."
> Colossians 4:6 (THE MESSAGE)

You will not be able to control all of the people who will offend you in your lifetime, but you can be intentional with your part in the conversations you have with others. Make a decision today that the goal of your future conversations and interactions will be to bring out the best in other people.

Give unedited compliments.

Point out the greatness in a friend.

Tell someone what they are good at; they may have forgotten or not realized it yet.

Remind them of a time they did something funny or impressive.

Go through their social media account and

like a few of their posts. Write a kind comment on it. It's not to be fake. It's to be *intentional.*

If we're honest, it's not difficult to criticize anything or anybody. It almost comes naturally to us. But what if we all chose to be better than that? For us to bring out the best in others in our conversations, we have to actually be *looking* for the best.

LABELS

Dealing with the part of us that criticizes others can be daunting. What can be even more daunting is dealing with the part of us that criticizes *ourselves.* Another defense mechanism we adopt is called, *self-criticism.*

This is the concept that if we can put ourselves down before anyone else can, it will give any offenses coming our way less of a punch. It's difficult for someone to make fun of you if you beat them to it.

Somehow, we believe the lie that if we can simply control where the offenses are coming from, they will have less of an impact on us. But self-destruction does not make the destruction any less *destructing*.

Regardless of whomever is doing the offending (whether it's you or another person), it still has the potential to rob you of your happiness and your God-given destiny.

There is an internal conversation that causes us to sway back and forth between being completely confident and completely insecure. When we are insecure about who we are, it will be remarkably easier to become offended, as opposed to when we are fully confident in our identity. As long as the question marks exist when asking who we are and who we are becoming, we will remain open targets for offense. To make matters worse, when we are insecure, we will continually strive to become whoever or whatever we assume other people will like the most.

There are four young men in the Bible, you might be familiar with, who we can learn from when it comes to knowing who we are. If you know the story, you will recognize them as Daniel and his 3 friends, Shadrach,

Meshach, and Abednego. Their story begins in the first chapter of Daniel.

Without giving you a complete Old Testament history lesson, allow me to give you the Cliffs Notes version of what's happening here:

Jehoiakim was the King of Judah. He was a king placed on the throne by the Pharaoh of Egypt who was being overthrown by Nebuchadnezzar, the King of Babylon. Nebuchadnezzar was the mighty ruler of the Babylonian Empire, taking over the Jewish culture. One of the first orders he gave under his new reign was to have all the children of Israel brought to him. Nebuchadnezzar not only apprehended the holy vessels from the temple, but he wanted to target Judah's future by alienating what historians believe were young men from the ages of 13-17.

During those times, a lot more than in today's society, there was a huge difference between the food enjoyed by royalty and the food commoners ate. Nebuchadnezzar knew the Jews were disciplined in their ways, so he used wine and royal meals to soften up the hearts and minds of these young men. Acceptance of the king's food was a sign of pledging loyalty to a kingdom.

Whoever they received their food from was considered their source.

They were in captivity while the king was trying to make them feel as though they were on vacation.

What happens next is something we need to pay close attention to. After the wining and dining, the king's chief eunuch changed their Hebrew names to Babylonian names.

The name **Daniel** (meaning *God is my judge*) was changed to **Belteshazzar** (meaning *Bel's prince*).

The name **Hannaniah** (meaning *Beloved by the LORD*) was changed to **Shadrach** (meaning *Illumined by Sun-God*).

The name **Mishael** (meaning *Who is as God*) was changed to **Meshach** (meaning *Who is like Venus*).

The name **Azariah** (meaning *The LORD is my help*) was changed to **Abed-Nego** (meaning *Servant of Nego*).

On a surface level, this doesn't seem like it's that big of a deal. But this transition completely challenged their identity in God.

Their new king wanted them to find their identity in *his* culture.

The same thing happens with us. Culture has a way of branding us by using categories and labels.

Rich.
Poor.
Black.
White.
Liberal.
Conservative.
Popular.
Introvert.
Extrovert.
Educated.
Single.
Married.
Divorced.

We've all had a label placed upon us that could potentially define our whole life.

But it doesn't have to.

BLACK AND WHITE

As a speaker, I get to talk to thousands of people at the same time from a stage without giving them the opportunity to talk back. People are allowed to form an opinion about me without being able to ask me a single question about my life. It comes with the territory.

Every now and then, there will be a well-meaning person who hears me speak and will tell me,

"Well, you're black on the outside, but you're really white on the inside."

It makes me wonder how they define *black* and how they define *white*.

How did they come to the conclusion I was white on the inside? I have heard people who are *not white* say they think life would be easier if they were--so should I be offended, flattered, or neither?

Is it the clothes I wear, the car I drive, the neighborhood I live in, or the cadence in which I speak that determines my ethnicity?

I grew up in a small, predominantly African-American Methodist church, and my dad was the pastor. Attending church wasn't optional for me. Neither was volunteering. My father frequently quoted, "*As for me and my house, we will serve the Lord!*" In fact, I'm not sure I even had the option of being saved! (I was ok with eternal security, so I didn't put up much of a fight on this one.)

Being a part of a smaller church, I had to learn how to do... well, everything. If the drummer decided not to show up (which was often), my brothers or I would have to fill in for the guy on the spot in front of 100 people and a choir. One time, the drummer was running late and my brothers were out of town, so it was my turn to learn how to play. As I slowly inched toward the drum set with two sticks in my nervously shaking hands, the drummer ran in the back door. Thank God. I can keep a beat, but drumming is not my calling.

All of our musicians played by ear and our song choices primarily came from one of two places: the first place was from a traditional book of hymns where everyone could turn to page 72 together and have a party. The second place was traditional for us, but perhaps a little unorthodox for most. My dad would loudly announce from the microphone, "Is there anybody here that has a song on their heart?" Then, random people from the crowd would come up and sing any song they felt like singing. Somehow, someway, we would all learn the song within seconds and we'd have the time of our lives. It was a free-for-all. It was basically Open Mic morning every Sunday, and we loved it.

Services for us started around 8:30am, sometimes. It all depended on what Sunday it was and how fast we had gotten ready as a family. It could be 9am, but overall, no one in our church was in a hurry. We would usually conclude our service around 12 or 1pm, but that was never a guarantee. Your best bet was to pack a light lunch just in case we were having too much fun.

I had an interesting upbringing because I was born in East St. Louis (which is not a place for the weak), but I went to school across the Martin Luther King, Jr. Bridge that went into St. Louis. So every single day, I commuted from the ghetto of East St. Louis, Illinois to the suburbs of St. Louis, Missouri. I lived and slept in one culture and was raised and educated in another. When my dad was transferred to a new church in Rockford, Illinois, it was of the same notion. My dad's church was located on the south side but I crossed a bridge to go to the east side where I attended a private school. Nearly every day of my adolescence, I crossed a bridge from one culture to another.

Unfortunately, when I was in 5th grade, my dad suffered a stroke that sent him into early retirement. During this season, my family had a lot of tough choices to make, including where we would all go to church. The school I attended at the time was connected to a large, predominantly Caucasian church where a lot of my friends went each weekend. Ultimately, my parents gave my brothers and I the choice to begin attending and getting plugged in there.

It was definitely a culture shift from my typical Sunday schedule. Service started at 9am sharp. When they said 9am, they weren't bluffing. At 8:59 the worship team was out there ready to roll; and without fail, when the clock struck 10am, the pastor would dismiss by saying, "Alright, thanks for coming today. We'll see you next week."

One hour?! Are you kidding me? I thought

we were just at the offering segment. You mean I can go home?

I had no idea what to do with myself, so I just sat there. Then somebody invited me to brunch. I said, "What in the world is *brunch*?" They said, "It's breakfast and lunch. You can get chicken or waffles...or both." I'm pretty sure I gave my life to Jesus at a brunch.

After high school, I began attending a culturally diverse church in downtown Chicago, a brand new experience for me. There were African-Americans, Caucasians, and Hispanics all singing to the same God, at the same time, in the same place. In all 18 years of my short life, I had never seen anything quite like that, and it changed the course of my future. Singing praises to God with all of those people made me wonder what worshipping in Heaven will be like.

I currently work at an extremely diverse church in Dallas, Texas. I serve on a leadership team with people who are of Assyrian, Lebanese, Italian, Tai, Puerto Rican, African American, Indian, Caucasian, Mexican, and Columbian descent, and then a bunch of others who are mixed with all of the above and more.

When I look back at all of the churches I have been a part of, with all the doctrinal differences and the theological chaos you get when you put them together, I realize individuals accepted Jesus into their hearts at every single one of them. The people in the black church, in the white church, and in the mixed church all had this one thing in common: Each church gave believers an opportunity to have an anchor for their soul. Each church gave people an opportunity to discover *Someone* who could change their life forever.

I was groomed in several ecclesiastical environments to not see the world through the color of my skin, my business degree, socioeconomic status, or accolades. Instead, I was given a perspective that reflects the heart of the Kingdom of God.

I was not taught not to see color. I was taught to see past it.

I was taught to appreciate the perspective of others who may not have grown up the way I had or may not believe what I believe.

People pull their identity from many different places.

Some like to be identified by their ethnicity or nationality.

Others like to be identified by their sexuality or political affiliation.

And others like to be identified by the way they dress.

But the way I see it, I can never be anything before I recognize myself as a Christ-follower, first and foremost. I am not a Black Christian. I am a Christian who happens to be African-American. The difference between the two is where I pull my identity from, and I pull it from following Christ. Everything else about me as an individual falls in line way after that. I perceive the world through a Christ-following lens above any other perspective some might want me to have.

Well-meaning people (and offensive ones) can put whatever label they want on me. They can place me into whatever category helps them understand me better. *But my soul has no color.* Call me what you want. It doesn't matter when I know who I am.

Daniel and his friends were given new names, but they did not allow new *labels* to change their character. They allowed their faith and integrity to be the attributes that made them stand out amongst their peers.

While Bible readers are familiar with Shadrach, Meshach, and Abednego more than they are with **Hannaniah, Mishael, and Azariah**, it's not their names which made them famous. The reason we still talk about them today is because of their courage to trust God while facing a fiery death.

One of my friends, who works as a youth pastor, recently had a group of his students write down the label they felt they wore the most. On a nametag that read, "Hello my name is _____", a handful of them wrote:

Failure.
Unwanted.
Nothing.
Hopeless.
Quitter.

Maybe you can relate. While I'm unaware of the specific label you carry, the question we have to ask ourselves isn't just, "Who am I?" but "Whose am I?" When you fully understand who you belong to and who died for you, you will never search for your self-esteem in the amount of love you can gain from other people.

Your capacity to be offended hinges on how you perceive yourself. If you view yourself and measure your identity by where you work, what you can afford, and your rising social media popularity, you will be enslaved to maintaining an image that demands to be constantly liked. That sounds exhausting. But when you see yourself through the lens of who Jesus Christ has made you to be, you anchor your identity in something and someone who does not, and will not ever change.

Food for thought:

1. How do you see yourself? Where do you pull your self-esteem from?

2. Is there someone you have offended without realizing it? (If you are struggling to think of someone, it could be the person you internally refuse to celebrate.)

3. Who do you need to celebrate?

MEASURING UP

Have you ever known someone who made you feel like a million bucks? Maybe it was a compliment that lifted you off the ground when they said, "Girl, that dress looks amazing on you. Have you lost weight?" Really, you just gained 5 pounds and now you're ready to buy them a house.

Have you ever played the let-me-see-if-I-can-get-all-of-my-groceries-from-the-car-to-the-house-in-one-trip game? Two trips is probably easier and smarter, but it's also weaker. Has my pride cost me smashed egg cartons from trying to carry 27 bags up 3 flights of stairs? Maybe. But I enjoy the workout and sense of accomplishment I feel when I walk through our door with our whole trunk hanging from every limb and finger I have.

If my wife sees my heroics and simply responds by saying, "How in the world did you bring all the groceries in already?"... I feel like an Avenger.

On the flipside, have you ever had someone make you feel worthless? Insignificant? Inferior?

Why is it so much easier to answer this question than the former? The answer is simply because we experience the opportunity to become offended much more often than we experience moments of encouragement. It takes a lot for us to feel encouraged and very little for us to feel discouraged.

Chances are, you were discouraged today. This could have happened on your way to church. This could have happened during your lunch break.

Maybe your kids did something to

discourage you as soon as you woke up.

Maybe your boss offends you every time you talk just by the way they *don't* listen.

Maybe you were offended by a passive aggressive comment from your spouse that only hints at how they really feel.

It could have been a sarcastic remark from a coworker. It might have been a joke dripping with the truth of what was really meant to be said.

It could even have been an offensive look or a feeling you get when you are around certain people. Discouragement gives us a keen awareness of what is wrong with us more than what is right with us.

It takes very little for us to feel as though we have failed as parents. It takes very little for us to feel as though we have missed the mark at work. It takes very little for us to feel as though we aren't good enough. Even when someone does try to encourage us, we often disregard or fight the compliment due to past offenses.

"You're doing a great job,"
collides with,
"No, I'm not."

"You look amazing today,"
collides with,
"But not yesterday?"

"That was pretty good for an old guy,"
collides with,
"So if I were younger, it would just be average?"

We can grow so accustomed to the offense of negative opinions; even the positive ones have trouble finding their way into our hearts. We get acclimated to darkness and it becomes hard to find the light. I've had a front row seat to seeing people who have allowed ONE negative opinion of them steer their entire life. It's as though they have put that one offense on repeat in their head as a somber reminder of why they'll never pursue their dreams.

People's opinions are like elevators. They can take us up, and they can take us down. They can build us up, and they can tear us down. If we're not careful, we will spend our lives chasing approval, trying to figure out ways to gain compliments and avoiding things that make people think negatively about us.

This mindset lands us in a place where we believe we are only good if other people say we are. We only look good enough if other people think we look good enough. Striving for the approval of other people will always cage you into feeling as though you need another person's permission to be who God has called you to be. **We spend way too much time looking for the approval of our gifts and talents from individuals who did not give us the gifts or the talents in the first place.**

When we live this way, it can feel as though the goal of our lives is to attain applause, as if being applauded is the antagonist to being offended. What's funny is, the plethora of *applause* has the ability to destroy your life just as much as *offense does*. As much as offense can leave you insecure, applause can leave you prideful. The return on investment from people's opinions isn't worth the stock you put into them.

<u>STRANGERS ON THE INTERNET</u>

We often feel as though we are missing the mark because we give other people's opinion of us the governing vote on how we are doing in life. Caring too much about what others think of us places the measuring stick in the hands of people who only see us in glimpses. If we can somehow get people to "like" our highlights on the Internet, then we can fool ourselves into believing they like *our whole life*.

If we can get friends and strangers on the Internet to love where we vacation, then we feel as though we are somebody special for 24 hours, until another one of our friends posts a better vacation spot. Inevitably, we continue to hand the measuring stick of success to other people, some of whom we don't even know and will never talk to. **The only way to stop caring about what people think of you is by giving the measuring stick to God.**

I believe Jesus gives us a phenomenal way to measure our lives. He does so by describing the Kingdom of God using a parable in Matthew 25. Here's what it says:

(ESV) Matthew 25:14 "For it will be like a man going on a journey, who called his servants and entrusted to them his property. [15] To one he gave five talents, to another two, to another one, to **each according to his ability.**"

Allow me to explain the currency scale in which Jesus is describing. A talent was a unit of weight of approximately 80 pounds. When used as currency for money, it was valued for that weight in silver. When a talent was used for money, it was worth about 6,000 denarii.

If you are not a mathematician, stick with me for a second.

A denarius was the usual payment for a **day's labor,** so the value of a talent was worth about 20 years of labor by an ordinary person. By modern standards (at the rate of the US minimum wage of $7.25 per hour), the value of a talent would be approximately $300,000 over 20 years, while at the median yearly wage of $26,363, a talent would be valued at about $500,000.

So if Jesus was sharing this parable today, he might say this was a manager who trusted one guy with $500,000, another with $2.5 million, and another with $5 million.

I love this because Jesus is telling us when we stand before God someday, our conversation will be all about what we did with what He gave us. **The measuring stick of success in the Kingdom is not based on being the best at what we do, but by giving our best with what we have been given.**

A key emphasis in this parable is Jesus says that this manager gave to "*each according to his ability.*" Here's why this is really good news for you and me: It means we never have to compare what we received with what anyone else has. It means whatever you were given is exactly what God thinks you can be trusted with at this time in your life.

You might want a new job. How hard are you working at your *current* one?

You might want a spouse. How do you treat your family, friends and current relationships God has already given you?

You might want more money. How are you stewarding what you already have?

We could easily measure our success or failure by our education or lack thereof, bank account, job title, relationship status, or social media followers, but God isn't measuring your life by any of those standards. He's measuring your life by seeing what you can be trusted with.

This frees you from being offended by people who don't think you're *being* or doing *enough*. Don't believe the lie that you will be good enough if and when you have a higher degree, six figures in the bank, CEO on the business card, happily married, or averaging 100 likes per post. **Strangers on the Internet don't get to decide if you are a success or a failure. God does**.

I know certain individuals who have allowed other people to set expectations for them beyond their ability. You can hang around some people who put pressure on you to spend money beyond your means, live in a house you cannot afford, or drive a car that costs you two paychecks just to get the oil changed. You can have work relationships where you are expected to do things outside of your capacity. If you want to live your life according to what God has enabled you to do, then a great question you should ask God right now is, **"Lord, what is my capacity?"**

A person can spend their entire life searching for what they were born to do and never understand their own capacity. I know stay-at-home moms whose husbands make enough for them not to work. I wonder how many times a week somebody says to them, "You're so lucky. You're living the dream." Perhaps, staying at home with the kids is somebody else's dream. What if that mom wants to work but feels as though she has to fit inside the stay-at-home mom box? It's natural for our joy to deplete when we are living somebody else's dream.

TWITTER'S MUTE FEATURE

My life became moderately more public when my wife and I got engaged and married on the same day. We filmed the entire proposal and wedding and put it up on YouTube, where it quickly went viral. Once *The Surprise Wedding* received over a million views, some people thought we were famous. It was never my intention to plan a surprise wedding to make us famous. I planned it because it was a desire of my wife's heart. I planned the wedding in secret for 2 years and couldn't even afford to have it filmed until 5 days before the big day. Viral was not in the "plans." Besides that, we were really only "famous" for one Thursday on Good Morning America until they ran Friday's show with more viral news.

Nevertheless, a million plus people got to experience our wedding, our vows, and our commitment and covenant of love to one another. A lot of people will see a million views on the documentary and miss the amount of negative comments and feedback directly below. There were some very mean and offensive comments I honestly don't remember because I turned off my notifications. However, I did hear about some of the negative comments through faithful friends of mine who would go onto the comment thread just to yell at the naysayers on my behalf. Now, those stories are hilarious to me.

A few months after our wedding, someone created a social media parody account, basically pretending to be "Ryan Leak" and mocking different parts of my life. He purchased a domain with my name in it and redirected it to a porn site. (He was a big fan.)

He then began tweeting famous pastors and speakers as "me" using inappropriate content. A few of them actually wrote me asking, "*Um, is this you?*" He twisted quotes from my sermons, utilized pictures from my real social media accounts, and then began to do his best to make "Ryan Leak" look bad. Oh, by the way, I know the guy. We went to school together. This was not a stranger.

The number one thing I wanted to do during this time was defend myself. I wanted to refute the statements he was saying about me. I wanted to set the record straight.

But what would my *defense* have accomplished?

I hadn't spoken to this guy in over a decade so I was unsure of what I had done to him that would make him do all of this. Regardless of what his reason was, it no longer mattered once I understood any defense I may have had about what I found offensive, would have just led to me *being offensive myself.*

How would *added* offense make his life or mine any better?

You may wonder what happened to him and the parody account. I honestly don't know. Twitter has a mute and block feature that keeps me from being able to see what the account posts.

If only our lives had the same features.

While you may not be able to fully block out and mute the opinions of others, you don't have to let them control your life. Just because someone did or said something with the intent to offend you, doesn't mean you have to dwell on it. An offense is designed to rob you of your happiness, and the longer you entertain the offense, the less happy you will be. Don't let one offense ruin your whole day, or allow one negative moment to govern your entire life.

When we are offended, we often feel as though we need to make major adjustments to our lives in order to avoid any future offenses. However, adapting your life to make other people feel better about your life only causes you to surrender to their opinion and offense. It would be as though you heard the offense and made a choice to agree with them or, at minimum, make you question who you are.

One of the many traps of offense is when it can cause you to spend your life trying to prove other people wrong.

You have nothing to prove! At the end of your life, you will not be measured by other people's opinion of you. So don't exhaust your energy trying to turn haters into fans. Spend your life focused on taking good care of what God has given to you. And that might mean you live a life that isn't that likable. It's more important for you to actually like your life more than the people who only see it in glimpses.

GOD'S STANDARD

In addition to the talents, resources, possessions, and relationships God has given us to steward, there is something else God has given us a particular measure of, which we also have to steward. It is found in the book of Romans, and here is what it says:

(ESV) Romans 12:3 "For by the grace given to me I say to everyone among you not to think of himself more highly than he ought to think, but to think with sober judgment, each according **to the measure of faith** that God has assigned."

In order for us to live unoffended lives, we have to start living our life by God's standards. The reason we get so offended and upset is because we feel as though we are not living up to a standard other people have created for us. God has given each of us a specific measure of faith, and can you imagine if discovering our exact measure of faith became our obsession? We would be less offendable because we would no longer seek someone else's approval of our life.

So let's recap. First, take a good, hard look at what God has entrusted you with currently. Secondly, evaluate the measure of faith you have been assigned. This is good news for you! Why? Because it's one thing to feel as though you are comparing your life and your possessions with other people's, but it's even worse when you feel as though your faith is being compared to someone else's.

Sometimes you can feel as though someone is more spiritual than you just because they have been going to church longer than you.

The almighty God has assigned you with a measure of faith and you have to ask yourself, *"What am I doing with the measure of faith I've been assigned?"*

We can spend a whole lot of time trying to impress other people, making sure they are pleased with us at all times. But how much time do we spend trying to make sure God is pleased with us? Ironically, the only way to make an impression on God is through faith. The Bible says it is impossible to please God without faith. One of the only times in the Bible you see Jesus raise an eyebrow, rather impressed, was when He saw a man's faith in Jesus' ability to heal someone in his circle just by speaking his belief out loud. Jesus said,

"Never have I seen faith like this in all of Israel."

If we cared more about what God thinks of

us rather than the opinions and beliefs of others, we would find ourselves growing in faith more than ever before.

To clarify, let me tell you what I am *not* saying:

"*Forget whatever the world, your friends, and your family says about you because THEY don't matter.*"

This is not about "them". This is about you regaining the authority from where and whom you get your confidence from.

People can have their opinion. It can be very beneficial to gain an outside perspective from people who can see things you can't. But today is about not letting another person's opinion of you dictate who you are. Perhaps you are reading this book right now because you gave life-defining authority to the wrong person years ago, and it's time to get your confidence back.

You will find yourself on the path to being unoffendable when you begin to allow God to set you free from slavery found in the court of public opinion. I encourage you to take your eyes off what people think about you and fix your eyes on what God thinks about you.

I believe it is crucial for believers to remind themselves of who they are on a regular basis, according to God's measuring stick. If you have been playing offenses on repeat in your mind, you need to replace the negative phrases with something positive—and there is nothing more positive than the Word of God. The truth of God's word will always serve as medicine for your heart, mind, and soul.

Here are a few statements derived from God's word that line up with what He thinks about you. If you are struggling with what people think about you on a daily basis, I encourage you to recite these statements out loud each day.

The Word of God says in Jesus Christ...
I am God's child (John 1:12)
I am Christ's friend (John 15:15)
I belong to God (1 Corinthians 6:20)
I am assured all things work together for good (Romans 8:28)
I am confident God will perfect the work He has begun in me (Philippians 1:6)

I have not been given a spirit of fear, but of power, love and self-discipline (2 Tim. 1:7)

I have redemption (Ephesians 1:8)

I am forgiven (Ephesians 1:8; Colossians 1:14)

I have purpose (Ephesians 1:9 & 3:11)

I have hope (Ephesians 1:12)

I am included (Ephesians 1:13)

I am alive with Christ (Ephesians 2:5)

I am raised up with Christ (Ephesians 2:6)

I am seated with Christ in the heavenly realms (Ephesians 2:6)

I am God's workmanship (Ephesians 2:10)

I am secure (Ephesians 2:20)

I am completed by God (Ephesians 3:19)

I have God's power (Ephesians 6:10)

I am victorious (I John 5:4)

I am protected by peace (Philippians 4:7)

I am chosen and loved (Colossians 3:12)

I am blameless (I Corinthians 1:8)

I am set free (Romans 8:2; John 8:32)

I am healed from sin (I Peter 2:24)

I am no longer condemned (Romans 8:1-2)

I am not helpless (Philippians 4:13)

I am overcoming (I John 4:4)

I am protected (John 10:28)

I am qualified (Colossians 1:12)

I am victorious (1 Corinthians 15:57)

Food for thought:

1. By what measuring stick do you define your success or failure?

2. Whose opinion really matters to you and why?

3. What are you doing with what God gave you?

4. How's your faith?

3

LIKE A GOOD NEIGHBOR

When I first got married, I learned very quickly I had a very specific way of doing just about everything and my wife had a very opposite, specific way of doing just about everything. I never knew dishwashers could be loaded in a different (and better) way. Nobody ever told me there was a different (and better) way to scramble eggs. To this very day, my wife and I use different toothpaste. She is a Colgate girl. I, on the other hand, don't have time for Colgate. Mentadent is my jam.

Now, marriage not only revealed to me I

have a specific way of doing things, but it continually reveals that my wife often has a *better* way of doing... well, just about everything. Her eggs are way better than mine. I love to clean, but she loves to DEEP clean. I have washed my face my whole life, but my wife has these facial masks that can deep clean your whole face like you have never washed it before. It's phenomenal.

But despite being "better" than me at certain aspects of life, the number one thing I want you to know about my wife is this: she is so stinking easy to love. You want to know who else is easy to love? Our son. I literally feel like it's Christmas morning when we get him out of his crib each day. (I know what you veteran parents are thinking right now. Just go with me for a second.)

What I know about you and me is this: it's relatively easy to love the people who love us back. It's similarly easy to *like* people who are *like* us. However, the people who have the greatest potential to offend us on a regular basis are the people who don't **look like, talk like, think like, believe like, vote like, spend money like, or live like us.**

We just spent the first two chapters of this

book discussing how to make adjustments regarding how we view ourselves. I believe the next step in becoming unoffendable is by altering how we view the world.

The best worldview we can have while living unoffendable lives is to choose to see the world through the eyes of our *neighbors*.

Jesus had a conversation with a lawyer in Luke 10 that gives us a great example of who our neighbors are, how we should treat them, and most importantly, how we should see *them*.

> **(ESV) Luke 10:25** "And behold, a lawyer stood up to put him to the test, saying, '**Teacher, what shall I do to inherit eternal life?**' **26** He said to him, 'What is written in the Law? How do you read it?' **27** And he answered, 'You shall love the Lord your God with all your heart and with all your soul and with all your strength and with all your mind, **and your neighbor as yourself**.' **28** And he said to him, 'You have answered correctly; do this, and you will live.'"

Love God. Love People. This mantra sort of simplifies the message of Jesus for us. Just love God and love people—and you'll be good to go.

There was a Macroeconomics course I took in business school that I found rather daunting. As a result of my disdain for the class, I found myself struggling with this course. One morning the professor invited me into his office to discuss my grades because he knew it was unlike me to struggle academically. He asked me if I was distracted by something away from the classroom. I played basketball in college, so he thought practices and games might have had something to do with it. I told him I felt I was doing better in the class than I clearly was, and maybe I had misunderstood the grading system. He understood, and graciously allowed me to redo one assignment before entering into finals. He was giving me an opportunity to fully apply myself and I was so grateful for the undeserved second chance, I eagerly picked up my bag and told him I would be back in the afternoon with the completed assignment.

He said, "Well, where are you going? If you didn't understand how to do it the first time, how are you going to complete it again by yourself? Let me teach it to you again."

I slowly put my bag down and took a seat. I was able to understand the material better in his office one-on-one than I was in the classroom setting. But had he let me run out of the office too early, I would have missed what I needed to learn.

I think we do this with scripture at times. We often leave the text too early and put periods where God puts a comma. If the takeaway from what Jesus first told this lawyer was just, "Love God and love people," then it would not be telling us the whole story. This lawyer's response is the one we should adopt.

> **(ESV) Luke 10:29** "But he, desiring to justify himself, said to Jesus, '**And who is my neighbor?**'"

This sentence is portrayed as though the lawyer is asking, if the requirement is to love God and love people, then our response should be, "*What* people?" Left to ourselves, we will often play our own referee deciding who is deserving of our love and who is *not*.

However, there are three fairly noticeable problems with the lawyer's question. The lawyer heard two commands, and quickly came to the conclusion he was good on the first one.

When we truly consider the depth of the first commandment, then who in the world has loved God

with *all* of their heart,

with *all* of their soul,

with *all* of their strength,

and with *all* of their mind?

We could all examine our hearts, souls, and minds to find margin where we have missed the mark on loving God in different areas. Nevertheless, this lawyer believed he loved God with all of his heart, soul, and mind, and therefore had no need for improvement on the first commandment.

However, his keeping of the second commandment depended completely on how Jesus defined who his **"neighbor"** was.

The second problem with the lawyer's question was in assuming he could fulfill the first command to love God without fulfilling the second command to love his neighbor. But loving God and loving people come as a package deal. We see this idea in 1 John:

(ESV) 1 John 4:20 "If anyone says, "I love God," and hates his brother, he is a liar; for he who does not love his brother whom he has seen **cannot love God whom he has not seen.** [21] And this commandment we have from him: whoever loves God must also love his brother."

Part of loving God with all of who we are is displayed in our lives through loving His creation. If this is true, it would be trivial to say,

"*We love God and we'll tolerate the people He created.*"

The third issue with the lawyer's reservation was in the desire to have the definition of "neighbor" dependent upon the convenience of his lifestyle. If Jesus' definition of neighbor were to include his family, friends, and lawyer colleagues, then perhaps this man would have fulfilled it. The Jews in Jesus' day did believe you had to love your neighbor. They had no problem being kind to their *kind*. But they were also taught it was, in fact, a duty before God to *hate your enemy*. We even see Jesus recognize this notion in the gospel of Matthew:

(ESV) Matthew 5:43 "You have heard that it was said, 'You shall love your neighbor and hate your enemy.'"

It all really depends on how a person differentiates between who their neighbor is and who their *enemy* is. Jesus chooses to answer this lawyer's neighbor question with a story:

(ESV) Luke 10:30 "Jesus replied, '**A man** was going down from Jerusalem to Jericho, **and he fell among robbers**, who stripped him and beat him and departed, leaving him **half dead. 31** Now by chance **a priest** was going down that road, and when he saw him **he passed by on the other side. 32** So likewise a Levite, when he came to the place and saw him, **passed by on the other side**. **33** But **a Samaritan,** as he journeyed, came to where he was, and when he saw him, **he had compassion. 34** He went to him and bound up his wounds, pouring on oil and wine. Then he set him on his own animal and brought him to an inn and took care of him. **35** And the next day **he took out two denarii and gave** them to the innkeeper, saying, 'Take care of him, and whatever more you spend, I will repay you when I come back.'"

ROADSIDE ASSISTANCE

As we examine this text, one of the first things we need to recognize is the road Jesus describes here is not a fictional setting. In fact, it is a road this specific lawyer would have been very familiar with. The road from Jerusalem to Jericho was notorious for crime and muggings. This road today is incredibly windy, having lots of twists and turns where it would be easy for robbers to have a positional advantage to surprise-attack their victims. The lawyer would not have been shocked Jesus would start off his story on this particular road.

In the story, a man has been stripped, beaten, and left almost dead on the side of the road. Jesus then introduces two more characters: a priest and a Levite. Both of these men represent religious officials who see their Jewish brother in obvious need of their help. But in Jesus' story, neither of them do anything. They both passed by on the other side.

We can assume they would have had logical excuses as to why they could not rescue the man in the moment. Perhaps they thought the road was too dangerous for them to stop and lend a helping hand. Maybe the guy was just pretending and he was actually a decoy.

The reality is, we all come face to face with needs we excuse ourselves from meeting. We will do our best to help someone in need as long as it is convenient for our schedule.

How many times have we driven past a car wreck and assumed someone else had already called 911? We use the assumption that the medical professionals have the situation under control, and therefore we conclude there is no need for us to help. But how do we actually know the situation is already taken care of if we never pull over?

Anyone with a car has experienced the moment when you exit a highway and see a person on the corner holding a sign with a request for help. The language on those signs has gotten really creative. It can almost feel like a sales pitch, and there are so many assumptions running through our minds when we see them.

"Do they really need money?"
"Is he really a military veteran?"
"Does he even have a family?"
"Are they telling the truth?"
"What will they do with the money?"
"I'm running late."
"I'm sure someone else will give to them."
"I don't have cash."
"They probably make more money than I do..."
"Did their house really burn down?"
"I'm not going to support their addiction."

One day, I came across a person in need on the side of the road and realized I didn't have any cash, but I did have this other thing in my wallet called a debit card. It allows me to go to a machine with money in it, and when I put in my secret PIN, it will spit out more than enough money to supply a meal for someone who needs it. The only issue here is taking the time for this extra errand would require an adjustment to my schedule.

But to be honest, I can only hope my faith is large enough to alter my schedule from time to time. I believe the gospel should inconvenience me more. I hope my life and schedule are not so full that I am unable to make space for God to use me in a moment. Nevertheless, I think we can all relate to the priest and Levite's logical reasoning for passing by on the other side.

Then Jesus introduces another character to the narrative. When this lawyer heard about the priest and the Levite, he probably expected Jesus to end the story by saying a common Jewish man came as the hero of the story to rescue the man left for dead.

Perhaps this would be another way Jesus would make a comparison between the religious elite and the commoners. Jesus often shed light on the corruption of the religious leaders, so the first half of this story feels as though it may be leaning in a direction beckoning us to root for the underdog. However, Jesus never introduced an underdog. He introduced an *enemy*. Jesus threw in a major plot twist by bringing in a *Samaritan*.

What we must understand about this culture and time period is Jews and Samaritans despised one another both racially and religiously. Based on cultural norms, the Samaritan would have had every reason to hate this Jewish man and keep on moving. Historians show us some rabbis actually taught that Jews were forbidden to help a Gentile woman who was in distress giving birth; because if they succeeded, all they would have accomplished was to bring one more Gentile into the world. They often thought Samaritans were *worse* than other Gentiles. It is plausible the Samaritan in this story would walk by and *actually rejoice* at seeing this Jewish man in agony.

But Jesus tells the lawyer, and us, that the Samaritan had something for this man he shouldn't have had: *compassion*.

He had the opposite reaction of what would have been considered normal. The man left for dead never asked for help, but the Samaritan did not need a request to respond. The Samaritan was the first responder. He was the first aid.

In one of his last messages at the end of the Civil Rights movement, Dr. Martin Luther King, Jr. stated the following regarding this text:

"The first question the priest asked, the first question the Levite asked was, 'If I stop to help this man, what will happen to me?' But then the Good Samaritan came by, and he reversed the question: 'If I do not stop to help this man, what will happen to him?'"

The wine the Samaritan had in this story, containing alcohol, would have helped to sanitize the man's wounds. The oil would have helped to ease his pain. Both of these remedies would have been a normal response for the man's external, medical needs. But to then put the man on his own animal would have meant the Samaritan himself would have been forced to walk. This is a man whose schedule and life had been inconvenienced completely.

Not only was his life inconvenienced, but Jesus also tells us he took out two denarii and gave them to the innkeeper where he brought the man to stay. The Samaritan's love for this man had now impacted his wallet! Biblical scholars would tell us two denarii would have provided for the man's needs at the inn for at least two or three weeks. He then tells the innkeeper if the man's bill exceeded what he had already provided, he would cover the extra cost when he returned.

This also shows us this Samaritan not only carried out a good deed for one day, but he intended on seeing how the man left for dead might recover. He exemplified extraordinary and sacrificial love for a man he should have hated.

Jesus concludes his lesson for the lawyer with this:

(ESV) Luke 10:36 "'Which of these three, do you think, proved to be a neighbor to the man who fell among the robbers?' [37] He said, '**The one who showed him mercy.**' And Jesus said to him, 'You go, and do likewise.'"

Jesus paints us a picture of a person who **proved** to be a neighbor to someone who lived outside of *their* neighborhood. In fact, Jesus paints a picture of a man who had an opportunity to help a stranger he had a lot of reasons to despise. **Jesus' conclusion in his explanation of who our neighbor is has less to do with our zip codes and more to do with our *comfort zones*.**

Perhaps "our neighbors" not only include the

people we like the most, share common interest with, and those who live in our neighborhood. Perhaps our neighbors are the people who don't look like, live like, vote like, act like, think like, believe like, or see the world like we do.

If we are being truly honest with ourselves, we have to admit we are often offended with people who don't see the world the way we do. We are offended by who they vote for. We are offended by the lifestyle they choose to live because it's not congruent with our own. When we believe it is our job to make others see the world the way we do, we will always be offendable. It's not our job to help our neighbors see the world the way we would like them to see it. It's our job to love our neighbors right where they are, without pre-qualifications.

Can you imagine a world where we extend loving arms to those who will never vote the way we do? Can you imagine a world where we live with enough margin to be able to pause our schedule for another person in need? What if we stop playing the referee of who deserves our sacrificial love and who will never be worthy of it? What if we begin living with the notion that whoever we come into contact with, wherever we come into contact with them, is a candidate for the grace and love shown to us by a Heavenly Father?

Jesus was focusing the microscope on the definition of who our neighbor is because he wanted to shed some light on the person we want to be our neighbor the least. By pointing this out, He invites us to push past our differences and live life like a good neighbor. Something powerful happens in our hearts when *they* and *them* become *we* and *us.*

Jesus doesn't need to tell us to love the people we already love. We don't need Jesus to be kind to our *kind.* He invites us outside of our comfort zone to show us what His love truly looks like.

Food for thought:

1. What needs exist in your corner of the world that you could help with?

2. Who is the hardest person or type of person for you to love?

3. Given Jesus' story, who do you think your neighbor is?

4. What item on your weekly schedule could you reduce to create space to help others?

HELLO FROM THE OTHER SIDE

Growing up in the 90s as the youngest of three boys, I was always jealous of my older brothers. They had jobs and I had an allowance. Their jobs afforded them a lot more shoes, clothes, and gadgets than my measly allowance did for me. One of the items I was the most envious of was their *pagers*. Some may have called them beepers.

It seems crazy these days to think back to a time before cell phones, but at one point in time, we kept change in our pockets at all times just in case we had to pull over to use a payphone. I would page one of my brothers and they would call the house 30-45 minutes later and only have enough change to talk for 2 minutes. Sometimes they would even use 1-800-COLLECT. (If you don't know what that is, ask your parents.)

It's odd to imagine it was once normal for us to not hear from one another for hours on end. Today, if someone doesn't text us back right away, or especially if they never text us back at all, we get offended. Do you want to know what the "true-friend" test really is? Put a friend on hold and take another call. If they stay on hold any longer than 3 minutes, they are the greatest friend you will ever have because most people are just too impatient to wait for you when they feel like you forgot they were even on hold!

If there is one person I can't stand texting with, it's my brother. I love him to death. But he has got to be the worst texter of all time. He is one of those one-word responding texters. He is simply not impressed with anything or anybody. One time, I had some very exciting news about getting to tryout for an NBA team. I thought to myself, the very first people I wanted to know about the biggest opportunity of my life would be my brothers, of course. I called him 3 times. No answer. Then he began a text thread with me I will outline for you in its entirety:

Brother: *Sup.*
Me: *Bro. You won't believe it, but I reached out to the Phoenix Suns and they're letting me tryout for the team on Monday man!*
Brother: *Coo.*

That's it. My brother couldn't even give me a full "cool" with an "L". He just gave me "coo." Love him.

Sometimes we will even become offended when the people in our world fail to give us a preferred response to something we feel is important. We can share our dream with a friend, and them simply not being impressed will make us feel distant. This can happen with a spouse. This can happen with an employer. Greater than any of those people... this can even happen with *God*.

What do you do when you feel as though God is not responding the way you want Him to? What do you do when you feel as though the person who has offended you the most is God Almighty? What do you do when you pray a big prayer for something near and dear to your heart... and God just says, "No," or you get no response at all? If we are being honest with ourselves and honest with God, there have been some days where an unanswered prayer has put some distance between Him and us.

If you have ever felt offended by God, the good news is you are not the first. There is a woman in the gospel of Matthew who I believe can relate. Matthew 15 says this:

(ESV) Matthew 15:21 "And Jesus went away from there and withdrew to the district of **Tyre and Sidon**. [22] And behold, a **Canaanite** woman from that region came out and was crying, 'Have mercy on me, O Lord, Son of David; my daughter is severely oppressed by a demon.'"

At the beginning of the text, the author, Matthew, leaves out the woman's name, but highlights her ethnicity. This woman is a Canaanite. This detail is important because it means she is a descendant of one of Israel's oldest rivals and enemies. And now she is walking up to a Jewish rabbi in need of a miracle. It should also be noted, historians tell us it was highly unlikely for Jesus to go to the region of Tyre and Sidon because

Tyrians had much ill will toward the Jews.

Considering her circumstance, it's not surprising this woman would lay down any ill will between their descendants to make her request. When we are desperate enough, it's amazing who we will gladly connect ourselves to in hopes of finding a solution. I'd bet you would gladly take a million dollars from the person you dislike the most. Nevertheless, this woman had a daughter who needed Jesus, and needed Him severely.

Given the racial tension in the text, she could reason Jesus may not want to heal her daughter simply because she was *not* a Jew. Clearly, she had heard stories of what Jesus could do. Perhaps this woman knew Jesus had healed Gentiles (non-Jews) before. We see evidence of this earlier in the book of Matthew in previous chapters. Yet what made this encounter special was Jesus performed those miracles as Gentiles came to Him on Jewish territory. Here, Jesus was meeting this woman on *her* territory.

Matthew continues the story with this:

(ESV) Matthew 15:23 "But he did not answer her a word. And his disciples came and begged him, saying, 'Send her away, for she is crying out after us.' **24** He answered, 'I was sent only to the lost sheep of the house of Israel.'"

Though this desperate mom pleaded for her daughter's life, Jesus' first response was not an encouraging one. The cry of her heart was met with silence. I don't know about you, but I have personally been there. I have had many moments where I felt as though I was leaving a voicemail for God wondering if my calls were going through. When you feel as though you are talking to a wall instead of God, it's extremely hard *not* to be offended.

After the silence, the disciples seemed rather irritated with the Canaanite woman. The act of sending her away could have one of two meanings: one meaning could be to send her away by healing the woman's daughter just so they could move on with their day; another meaning could be to send her away with nothing so they could still move on with their day. Regardless of the intentions of the disciples, neither response makes this woman feel better about who she is to Jesus or who Jesus is to her.

To make matters worse, Jesus' first words in this story are, *"I was sent **only** to the lost sheep of the house of Israel."*

This is the opposite of good news for this mom. In fact, this is opposite of everything she had probably heard about Jesus up to that point. The odds were definitely stacked against a mom who simply had nowhere to take her daughter. She was one Gentile woman taking on 13 Jewish men and the only thing she wished she could be in this moment was *Jewish*. If she could just be a part of the house of Israel, she would have been a qualified recipient of a miracle. So what in the world could she do?

We've all been there ourselves. We've all had a moment or two in our lives where we thought God would answer our prayers if we had just been in church a few more times, or prayed a specific prayer more often. In these moments, it can feel as though there is an exclusive country club for those who get prayers answered, and if your spiritual resume is not up to par, there is no way to be with the *in* crowd.

But Matthew gives us this woman's astounding response here:

(ESV) Matthew 15:25 "But she came and knelt before him, saying, 'Lord, help *me.*'"

This woman pushed past the perceived rejection of 13 Jewish men. She could not solve the racial tension between her past and theirs, but she could do something about her daughter's severe condition.

Notice, she did not pray,

'Lord, help my daughter,'

but,

'Lord, help me.'

Something amazing happens when we lament for other people. It's about having the ability to feel what somebody else is feeling and allowing *their* pain to be *our* pain. While this mother is becoming more endearing to us, it only gets worse before it gets better.

(ESV) Matthew 15:26 "And he answered, 'It is not right to take the children's bread and throw it to the dogs.'"

Um. Excuse me, Jesus. Did you just refer to

this woman as a *dog*? At this point in the story, I am offended for this mom and embarrassed for the disciples. If I were a disciple here, I would be thinking... *I get we have things to do, places to go, and people to see, but I was not aware we were making dog references in response to requests for miracles. I thought one of the central themes of our ministry is compassion. No?*

JESUS WALKS

Can you imagine how this mom felt? You would think this woman would have simply walked away disappointed with the fact Jesus did not come as advertised. You would think this Canaanite would have chalked off this perceived insult and offense merely as bad blood between her people and His. But here is what she actually did:

(ESV) Matthew 15:27 "She said, 'Yes, Lord, *yet even* the dogs eat the crumbs that fall from their master's table.' **28** Then Jesus answered her, 'O woman, great is your faith! Be it done for you as you desire.' And her daughter was healed instantly."

Wait a minute. Jesus wasn't giving her an insult. He was giving her a test. He was seeing how far her faith would take her if she were faced with obstacles. He wanted to know if she had the capacity to take a hit and keep going. It was as though she had said,

"Jesus, I understand the primary focus of Your ministry is to the Jews and they have a special place in God's redemptive plan. Yet I also understand Your ministry extends beyond the Jewish people, and I want to be part of Your extended blessing."

These were two incredible words full of faith: **Yet even**. She accepted Jesus' description of her and asked for mercy despite it. Maybe she asked for mercy because of it. *"Yeah, even dogs need help too."*

This woman had a profound ability to be unoffendable. This woman had an uncanny ability to look past the racial and cultural labels, even Jesus put on her to examine her heart, and saw herself as a simple mom with some great faith.

The greatest test of our faith can be found through being offended. Anytime you are faced with an offense, make a choice to view it as a litmus test of your character to reveal if you really believe God is for you. The first chapter of Peter says this:

(ESV) 1 Peter 1:7 "These trials will show that your *faith is genuine.* It is being tested as fire tests and purifies gold—though your faith is far more precious than mere gold. So when your faith remains strong through many trials, it will bring you much praise and glory and honor on the day when Jesus Christ is revealed to the whole world."

On the other side of a trial and on the other side of an offense is a blessing. This Canaanite woman's faith was so amazing we don't even know her name. The only thing we know about this woman is her address and her faith. She was humble, patient, persevering, and obviously winning the mom-of-the-year award. Yet Jesus didn't compliment any of those good things. Instead, He brought attention to her faith. She flipped Jesus' words inside-out and turned an insult into an *opportunity* to build her faith.

This woman could have walked away after the first offense, because that is what we often do. I know people who have walked away from God because of one perceived offense from God or one of His followers. But if this woman would've walked away too soon, she would have missed her miracle. And you will too. Some people walk away from God because of one unanswered prayer and miss out on a whole life of blessing that God has for them. Don't let that be you.

Now here's the best part of the story...

> **(ESV) Matthew 15:29** "Jesus *went on from there* and walked beside the Sea of Galilee. And he went up on the mountain and sat down there."

The region of Tyre and Sidon were Gentile cities, located some 50 miles away. The Bible has no record of Jesus doing anything else in Tyre and Sidon besides this encounter with this woman.

Jesus went 50 miles out of His way to meet this one Gentile woman's need.

This shows remarkable and unexpected love from Jesus toward the woman of Canaan in how He would go out of his way to make a point for individuals who don't feel like they're on the inside track when it comes to church.

"Hey God, I'm not on the VIP list. I'm new. I'm on the outskirts of what it seems like you're doing." That's ok, because *Jesus walks*.

I am not aware of all you have heard about Jesus. Maybe you would recognize His wedding party trick of turning water into wine. Maybe you have heard of how He acts at picnics with 5,000+ starving people when He gave everybody and their mom a fish dinner. Maybe you have lived under the pretense that church is only for people who are well-versed and have their act together. While I would love to change that perception of the church, I would rather tell you no matter how far from God you feel... *Jesus walks*. And there is no distance He wouldn't go for you.

Offenses have the ability to either destroy your confidence or to build your faith. God wants to use every offense you have ever experienced from other people, and maybe even Him, to build your faith and bring you closer to Him. Just because you were given an offense, does not mean you have to take it. On the other side of an offense, you will be able to look back and realize it was something that could make you better, not bitter. That is what happens when the love of Jesus walks into your life.

Food for Thought:

1. Have you ever been offended by God?

2. Do you feel as though you can be honest with God?

3. Are there trials in your life that you now look back on, realizing they made you (or are making you) better?

4. Are there some things in your life that have caused distance between you and God that perhaps God wants to use to bring you closer to Him?

YOU CAN HANDLE THE TRUTH

One of the things I love the most about kids is they are the most honest people you can find. They have yet to learn the concept of living life with a filter and are completely unaware of when or how they are offending you. I have 4 nieces who always keep it all the way real with me when I have not requested their input. I remember the first time I ever bought black skinny jeans. I put them on and one of my nieces said,

"Why are you wearing leggings?"

I said, *"They're JEANS."*

She said, *"Looks like leggings to me."* She had a point.

Another time I had a niece ask me, *"Why are your friend's teeth so yellow?"* They really are wonderful children who love Jesus.

As adults, we learn appropriate filters (most of us) for cordial conversations, but every now and then we will run into a friend who wasn't given the gift of encouragement. Even their compliments are offensive, as if an asterisk comes with every affirmation.

"You actually look great today."
*We note the words **actually** and **today**.

"You started working out? Praise God."
*Did you have to praise God about it though?

One time a lady came up to me at the end of a church service and told me I did such a good job that she took notes on all of the things I said *wrong* so I could do even better next time. (Thank you?) One person heard me speak at a conference and told me I had gotten A MILLION times better since the last time they heard me. (God bless you too?)

The strategy of the enemy is to destroy every relationship you have, *one offense at a time.*

If we allow offenses to linger, it could take years, even decades, to realize how far you and someone you love have drifted apart. I know married couples who have woken up 10 years into a very unhappy marriage asking themselves how they got there. They arrive *there* one offense at a time.

The enemy works hard to create negative space in our marriages, our friendships, and our working relationships. Sadly, the offense often stems from something that was never *intended* to hurt the other person, though it was received that way. Offenses can feel as though a person is trying to hurt you when they may just be expressing how much they have been hurt and lack the ability to communicate pain in a healthy way.

THAT PERSON

When it comes to some of our closest relationships, I believe there are times when what we find offensive and destructive can actually be beneficial and constructive. If we are going to have successful careers, marriages, and lives, we must learn how to receive the truth without being offended by it.

What I know most about the people who love you is this: **they find it incredibly difficult to be honest with you.**

Why? Because hurting your feelings is the last thing they want to do. I can prove it. I guarantee there is at least one person in your life you feel as though you can't be honest with because of how they will respond.

Maybe the person is your boss, and you would really like to stay employed.

Maybe it's your spouse, and you have calculated that telling them the truth might equal making your marriage worse.

Maybe it's your best friend, and they can only handle little bits of truth at very specific times. It is obviously someone you love and respect, but because you know them so well, you have had a front row seat to see how they have responded to honesty before—and it did not go well. What you and I need to realize is we all have the potential to be *that* person.

On some level or another, I believe every single one of us is self-deceived. We have all convinced ourselves to believe we are too good at something or too bad at something. Without the perspective of other people, we will always err on one side or the other. Without having made the space for people to be genuinely honest with us about our lives, we will always live either overly confident or insecure.

The best way for you to receive honesty is **by invitation-only**. Uninvited honesty will always sound like criticism. You will never be able to control if and when other people will invite you to be honest with them, but *you can* control the people you invite to be honest with you. And what they have to tell you is a truth you can handle.

Know this, when you invite someone to be honest with you, your response to what they have to say will determine if they will ever be honest with you again. If you get offended and defensive, you will close the door on future honest conversations.

We have all worked for bosses who thought they were good bosses who were not good bosses. We have all had friends who thought they could sing who were not blessed with vocal talent, yet expect you to drive them to American Idol auditions. We all know people with anger issues who are unable to recognize how mad they get over the smallest issues. We have all had people we love with addictions who believe they have *it* under control when *it* is controlling them. We have all clearly seen a blind spot in another person's life, and yet we did not feel as though we had the license to tell them. The question we have to answer is this: **How do we know if we are *that* person?**

The only way we are ever going to know if we are *that* person is if we **invite** someone or some people into the sacred space of our lives and ask them to give us the honest insight and perspective we are unable to see on our own.

Here are a few things people find it the most difficult to be honest with you about: your romantic relationships, your kids, and your passion. Anything you have an emotional attachment to will be a sacred cow in your life people are afraid to touch. I can prove it.

How many times have you had a friend who was dating somebody you knew they should not be dating, but you let them date them for 6 months anyway? When they finally broke up, you finally told them, "I never thought they were good for you anyway." Why were you unable to be honest with them for 6 months? Because they were falling in love and refused to see from the inside what you could clearly see from the outside.

If you have children, a protective filter is attached to your perspective the minute they join the planet. No one can talk about your son or daughter. But what if somebody else can see something about your kid that you are unable to see because of this filter? We have all been around some children where we saw some negative behavior and wondered how their parents would deal with it, yet said nothing because our perspective was not invited. What I know about you and myself is we all can clearly see the flaws of others with an outside perspective but can often be blinded to our own flaws from the inside.

If you have people who work for you, invite them to be honest with you.

If you have someone you work for, invite him or her to be honest with you.

If you're married, invite your spouse to be honest with you.

Ask a friend who has a front row seat watching you live to give you perspective. It could be about **what you do** or **who you are**. Make it hard for yourself to get offended by setting them up to win in the conversation. Not only ask them what they really think about you or something you do, but ask them how who you are or what you do could be *better*.

A person who loves you will not want to hurt you, so assist them in the process of getting honest feedback from you. If they feel as though they are going to hurt you, most of the time, they will call an audible and say nothing or tell you what you want to hear. But if you can make them understand they are helping you become better at who you are or something you do, then what good friend wouldn't want to help a friend get better?

One of my friends recently asked me if I saw any red flags in a new relationship they were entering into. I responded with,

I don't see any red flags but I see a few yellow lights.

I simply saw a few areas where they should *proceed with caution.*

But if I was inclined to offer my perspective without an invitation, the space for them to be offended is enormous.

FRIENDLY FIRE

While what honest friends might say may sting in the moment, it's better to receive helpful criticism from someone who cares about you than from someone who does not have your best interest at heart. Proverbs 27 says this:

(NIV) Proverbs 27:6 "Wounds from a friend can be trusted, but an enemy multiplies kisses."

One of the many people who consistently give me authentic and genuine perspective is my best friend, James Wilson. He will always be someone I allow to be somewhat of a referee in my life. He always helps me make calls on things I am unable to see all the angles on. There are days when I call him just to get permission to be mad. Sometimes he listens and agrees. Sometimes he listens for an hour and slowly lets me know I am just flat out wrong.

One of the short films I recently created is called, *Chasing Failure*. In this documentary, I answer the question, "What would you do if you knew you couldn't fail?" My answer was being in the NBA. The point of it all was to encourage people to know they don't have to let the fear of failure keep them from pursuing their dreams. Long story short, I was given an opportunity to try out with the Phoenix Suns for two days. You can go to chasingfailure.com and watch the whole thing if you would like to.

Spoiler alert: I failed.

When and if you watch it, you will see the documentary is about 15 minutes in length. But it was not always this way.

The first draft of *Chasing Failure* was approximately 30 minutes long, and one of the first 5 or so people who I showed it to was James because I wanted to know what he thought. The first 4 people who saw it raved, "Man, I love it! It's amazing." But I knew James would give me a more detailed perspective. I trust his eye. He watched the whole thing and at the end he asked, "How done do you think it is?" I said,

"About 85-90%."

He responded, "25%".

He then gave me a list of things that would make it better. If I am being honest, I was emotionally attached to my work and I was very offended. I had spent so many hours editing the first draft and in that moment, I felt like he just ripped it to shreds. I went from being offended to just being downright discouraged.

A few days later, I began editing the film some more and I realized he was completely right. It was way too long. Subtitles were needed in spots where I was not wearing a microphone. When he first gave me his critiques, I was so emotionally connected to the project that I was blind to what could make it better. But once I was finished with it, I was really able to thank him for being honest with me.

If we invite people close to give us honest perspective and then hold on to bitterness because they did exactly what *we* asked them to do, we will never truly grow. For example, let's discuss the person who told me I had gotten a MILLION times better since the last time they heard me speak. I really had to think about it for a few days to understand why I was offended by that comment when, in all reality, my goal as a communicator is to get better every time I speak. I am constantly working on my craft. So that person's comment is confirmation and affirmation I am reaching my own personal goal of getting better. So why was I offended?

Another time, I asked my friend, Alan, if he saw any blind spots in my life. Over and over and over again, he would tell me he didn't see anything at the moment. After I bugged him enough, he finally spit it out, "Well if I'm being nitpicky... you walk really fast."

I thought, "Huh? What do you mean I walk really fast? What kind of blind spot is that?" I actually said out loud, "Ok... explain..."

He explained to me, I can be very intentional and very busy, and sometimes those two things can work against each other. He gave me an example of a time where I stopped and intentionally had a conversation with someone, and it made their day. He then gave me another example of when I was in such a hurry to do something important that I walked right past the same person and ignored them completely. He encouraged me to slow down more often so I could really see people.

Before that conversation, if you had asked me to share with you one of my weaknesses, I would never have said, "I'm a really fast walker." But Alan allowed me to see I could be perceived from other people in a way that is contrary to the person I desire to be. Another friend put it a different way when he told me, "You have the ability to be the most engaging person in a room, and you also have the ability to be the most *disengaging* person in a room—and the room can feel it when you do either one."

I could not be more grateful for their perspective because positive feedback is exactly what allows me to grow and become the best version of myself. The more unoffendable I become, the more I leave space for people to help me see what I can't see on my own.

Even Jesus asked His disciples about his reputation amongst the people:

(NLT) Luke 9:18 "One day Jesus left the crowds to pray alone. Only his disciples were with him, and he asked them, 'Who do people say I am?' **19** 'Well,' they replied, 'some say John the Baptist, some say Elijah, and others say you are one of the other ancient prophets risen from the dead.' **20** Then he asked them, '**But who do you say I am?**' Peter replied, 'You are the Messiah sent from God!'"

Jesus had a moment where he checked the pulse of public opinion about who he was, and the people had an inaccurate interpretation. But his best friend got it right. You will have people in your life who will inevitably misunderstand who you are, but there needs to be someone or some people in your life who can help you navigate moments when your confidence is shaken.

THE OPPORTUNITY
OF OFFENSE

What I know about you and myself is this: we will never be in a position where we will be completely protected from offense because we simply can't control what other people say about us. But we can control what we do with what people say about us.

One of the biggest mistakes made in managing offenses is in believing **one person's** opinion is **everybody's opinion**.

So if one person says you were unsatisfactory in your work, you go home and believe the entire company thinks you are a horrible employee. You could be one customer-complaint away from a midlife crisis.

There is even a chance one person's opinion has been controlling how you have lived your entire life. I know people who heard one offensive remark in middle school that caused them to obsess over their weight for decades. They made one opinion everyone's opinion by assumption, and now continue to live their lives responding to the comment of a person they most likely have not spoken to in 20 years.

Offenses are pivotal for your growth as a person. If what makes you feel offended is true, then now you know the areas in which you can get better. If it is false, it should give you more confidence that what you are doing and who you are becoming can take punches and keep going. Either way, you are winning because you are choosing to win. This is vital for becoming unoffendable. This allows you to live in a world where you make the choice to take an offense on the chin and use it for your own personal development. That is a choice most people are not willing to make, but it is a choice that will make a difference between being healed and staying broken.

The question you have to ask yourself is this: Who do you have in your world that is honest enough, and loves you enough to help you determine who and what opinions you should adhere to and what opinions should be rendered invalid? The only way you can begin being unoffendable is by inviting people into your life to be painfully honest with you.

Here's one way the Bible shows us how these relationships can look for us:

(ESV) Ephesians 4:15 "Rather, **speaking the truth in love**, we are to grow up in every way unto him who is the head, into Christ, **16** from whom the whole body, joined and held together by every joint with which it is equipped, when each part is working properly, makes the body grow so that it builds itself up in love."

This verse shows us, truth in love can build us up. Sometimes we can believe the lie that if people really love us, then they will tell us what we want to hear. We live in a world where we want people to tell us we are good at things we are actually *not* good at because we have adopted the notion that if we encourage someone enough they will eventually live up to what we have praised them to be. Maybe. Maybe not.

Finding out what we're *not* good at actually helps us narrow down what we should spend most of our energy working on. While the gap remains between what we believe people can be and their actual reality, we all need to come to grips with the truth. Just imagine what we could become with a lot of encouragement AND the truth.

Another way to set your loved ones up to win, when you ask them to help you get better, is by making sure you don't put pressure on them for the exercise to be reciprocated. In other words, once they tell you what you can get better at, you will automatically think of a thousand things they can work on as well. You may feel as though this is your way of evening the score so you can both go home and have something to work on. This exercise requires humility. For now, leave them out of it. You might want to say something back to them out of feeling offended rather than true love for them. Remember, when you are asking for honest feedback from someone who loves you, walk into those conversations with humility, and fight the propensity to want to defend yourself.

Sometimes we only want to receive perspective and correction from someone who is an authority above us or from someone who we believe is better than us at our craft. For example, as a public speaker, I tend to lean toward paying the most attention to feedback from other public speakers.

That would be a mistake.

As a writer, I tend to only value the opinion of other respected authors.

That would be a mistake.

Why? *Because I don't write messages or books for other speakers and authors.* I don't speak for the sake of other public speakers and communicators. So why would I shun the perspective of the people who actually listen to my messages and read my books?

Another example of this was when I recently had a friend ask me for marriage advice. He has been married for almost 20 years, while I have only been married for 4 years. Furthermore, he faithfully coordinates a successful marriage class for a church. I should be getting counsel from him. But what impressed me most about his honest inquiry was that he does not believe he has arrived at a place where he is unteachable. When a veteran is willing to learn from a rookie, both parties have the opportunity to get better.

When you have honest conversations with someone you love, you will want to listen intently. What qualifies them to speak into your life is the fact that they love you. It has nothing to do with them being better than you. If you become offended and genuinely believe they are wrong, humbly take what they said to a second trusted friend and see if they agree or disagree. **An even better idea is take it to God in prayer**.

If a friend points out you have a tendency to overreact in certain situations, ask God if unresolved anger is something in your life that needs work. If an employee points out you micromanage a lot of other employees and processes, yet you believe the opposite to be true, ask God if you have room for improvement in your life as a leader. If a spouse lets you know your sarcasm can sometimes come across as rude and inconsiderate, ask God if there is room for improvement regarding what you allow to come out of your mouth.

From my experience, there is generally some percentage of truth in every criticism we receive and it would be wise of us to choose to grow and become better for every single one of them. **Your greatest opportunity to learn is the next time you find yourself offended.**

I am almost positive you can think of some people who you would love to be honest with, but you cannot control other people's openness to truth in love. You can only control your own invitations, and when you invite perspective in, you are giving yourself an opportunity of a lifetime to maybe hear the truth for the first time. And it is a truth I believe you can handle.

Food for Thought:

1. Who exists in your life that can tell you the whole truth and nothing but the truth?

2. When people try to give you perspective, how do you respond?

3. How are you currently managing negative opinions?

4. Who do you need to invite into your life to be honest with you?

MARGIN FOR ERROR

When my wife and I were expecting our first child, we were given the advice to go to a pregnancy class to help rookie parents learn what to do. At this point, I'm not sure if it was our pride or our schedule, but we never made it. Overall, I felt as though taking care of an infant couldn't be THAT hard.

Then our son arrived.

A few days later, I was doing the thing we all do when we don't know what to do: Googling it. What was "it" you may ask?

Everything.

I found myself YouTubing how to properly swaddle an infant. And don't get me started on car seats. They have the complex features of luxury vehicles these days. At one point, I was using a syringe to drip milk into this boy's mouth. I had no idea what in the world I was doing, but thank God for my wife. She naturally knew what to do without instructions. (She keeps our family alive.)

We didn't feel bad about being rookie parents until we got around some veteran parents. Now, I have understood and played the adult comparison game regarding clothes, cars, and houses, but it was not until I walked into a store called BuyBuyBaby, for all things baby, that I was made aware of the "baby stuff" comparison game. Did you know you can have a Keurig for your baby's milk? You can make a coffee for yourself and a perfectly warm milk for your baby in just 60 seconds. Walking through BuyBuyBaby made me feel as though our parenting was being measured by the quality of our stroller. Believe me, there is a Range Rover of strollers out there.

I will never forget my first conversation with

some veteran parents when I began describing our deprivation of sleep. The struggle was real. The veteran parent just looked at me and said, "You guys didn't go to the parenting class?" I said, "Nope." She then asked me if we had purchased a list of items "ALL parents know about" in some apparent user guide you get when you have a child that we clearly never received.

I was not only offended by the way this veteran was not operating with more grace in their life, but I was also waiting for her to compliment us on how our son looked.

Can we keep it real for a second? Everyone believes they have the cutest baby in the world, but that is veeeeeery objective. We are all beautiful in the eyes of God, but I am not Him. I am also not the Cute Baby Police, but as a parent, you find yourself waiting for someone to comment about your baby, and when they fail to do so, you feel slightly offended. Or you can become really offended when you hear the same person complimenting somebody else's baby.

In our minds, by calling somebody else's baby cute, you just called my baby ugly.

It is silly really, but we all have the tendency to play mind games that cause us to come to some rather odd calculations about ourselves and about other people.

The biggest offenses some of us will have in our lives will actually come from two surprising places:

What people **never say to you** and what you hear people say to others you **wish was said to you**.

We all have the propensity to live an offendable life because of these two things. The greatest test for your confidence is to hear somebody else be complimented on the same thing you do. It can be hard to see somebody else being adored, noticed, recognized, and rewarded for something you do a lot of and they do very little of. I call this *phantom discouragement*. No one actually said anything negative about you. But watching someone else be paid a compliment feels like it cost you something.

Maybe phantom discouragement showed up when your boss highlighted a co-worker's hard work and gave them a raise. You do more than them and your boss could care less, making you feel overlooked.

Maybe you have a really good-looking friend who consistently gets compliments every time you go out together, but nothing is said about you.

Maybe you went through a really tough time when you lost a job, a marriage, or a loved one, and you kept track of all the people who failed to reach out to you when it happened. You have an on-going tally of who has called you since and who hasn't.

Maybe you have a parent who always seems to be impressed with everybody else but you.

Maybe you know a pastor who preaches about love behind the pulpit, but never responded to your email. Offenses easily come when we realize somebody we expect to be a perfect representation of Jesus is actually just a flawed follower of Him.

The issue is not that we have a real problem with other people being complimented, but **phantom discouragement will put a negative spin and filter on everything positive around us that is *not about us*.** This will lead us to being offended by the people we love the most and who love us back.

HEY SAUL

We are not the first people to deal with phantom discouragement. Here is what happened with a guy in the Old Testament named Saul:

(ESV) 1 Samuel 18:6 "As they were coming home, when David returned from striking down the Philistine, the women came out of all the cities of Israel, singing and dancing, to meet King Saul, with tambourines, with songs of joy, and with musical instruments. **7** And the women sang to one another as they celebrated, '**Saul has struck down his thousands, and David his ten thousands.**' **8** And Saul was very angry, and this saying displeased him. He said, 'They have ascribed to David ten thousands, and to me they have ascribed thousands, and what more can he have but the kingdom?' **9** And **Saul eyed David from that day on.**"

Saul allowed the praise of David to become the demise of his confidence. He allowed himself to become offended by what was actually a compliment to him. His envy became poison to his calling.

Saul, what is so wrong with being a person who has struck down thousands? If you are going for the warrior type of compliment, you are in good company.

Saul eyed David from that day on. Saul lost sight of who he was and set his sights on who he needed to be better than. Here's what the Bible said about Saul nine chapters before his downfall:

(ESV) 1 Samuel 9:2 "And he had a son whose name was Saul, a handsome young man. There was not a man among the people of Israel **more handsome** than he. From his shoulders upward he was **taller** than any of the people."

Hey Saul, you are notably the best-looking guy in the land... according to the BIBLE! When movie stars get voted as "Sexiest Man Alive" by a magazine, it is really a matter of popular opinion. But if the Bible says there is nobody better looking than you, then you're top shelf. Not to mention, you're taller than everybody too. So not only are you really good looking, but everyone gets an opportunity to know and see you on a regular basis because of your height. Yet you allowed one song from a group of women to make you forget who you already were.

You would assume it was enough for Saul to be continuously complimented on his good looks and ability to strike down thousands, but those truths became irrelevant when he shifted his focus onto the praises of David. When praises for David were all he focused on around him, criticism was all heard inside him. It polluted his thinking and drove him mad.

The Bible gives us a great example of how to handle the praises and successes of other people. However, this time it is not between Saul and David; it is between John the Baptist and Jesus.

To give you the background story between these two, John the Baptist is Jesus' friend and cousin. When John the Baptist baptized Jesus, the heavens opened up and God declared his love and approval for Jesus right then and there. John began his ministry earlier than Jesus and therefore acquired more disciples before Jesus even got started. Because of John's growing ministry, most people would come to John for baptism and repenting. But as Jesus began His ministry, things began to change.

> **(NLT) John 3:25** "A debate broke out between John's disciples and a certain Jew over ceremonial cleansing. **26** So John's disciples came to him and said, 'Rabbi, the man you met on the other side of the Jordan River, the one you identified as the Messiah, is also baptizing people. And **everybody is going to him instead of coming to us**.'"

Essentially, John's disciples are telling John that Jesus is taking all of their baptism business. Baptizing was John's deal. It is what he is known for. And now people are choosing to go to Jesus over John. In today's context, it could be compared to the idea of people deciding they want to go to Jesus' church instead of John's. The report given to John by his disciples about Jesus sounds just like the song Saul heard about David. The difference with John is how he responded to the rise of Jesus.

(NLT) John 3:27 "John replied, 'No one can receive anything unless God gives it from heaven. **28** You yourselves know how plainly I told you, 'I am not the Messiah. I am only here to prepare the way for him.' **29** It is the bridegroom who marries the bride, and the bridegroom's friend is simply glad to stand with him and hear his vows. **Therefore, I am filled with joy at his success. 30** He must become greater and greater, and I must become less and less.'"

According to John, if someone has been given success, God gave it to them for a reason. **The success God gives someone else does not have to dictate how happy you are with yours.**

John shows us it is possible to have less success than other people and still be happy about it. He even shows us perhaps more joy can be found in *less* success for us. Real joy is not when you can be happy for your own success, but when you can be happy for others as well. Some people can only celebrate other people as long as their life is a little bit more successful than those they are comparing it to. Don't let that be you.

John could have had his eye on Jesus and let the praises of Jesus' growing ministry make him feel as though his own ministry was insignificant.

Saul's destiny was altered all because of one offensive moment. Saul let what he wanted to hear being sung about him drive him away from who he was called to be. He was already amazing and anointed, but he was blinded to his own worth because of his jealousy of David. What if you're currently blind to the thing you're great at because you're too busy focusing on the gifts and talents of others?

Is it feasible that there are people in your life who love you and compliment you all the time and you don't even hear it because you are *waiting* to get a compliment from one specific person you will never hear it from?

Sometimes we not only want to be encouraged, but we want to be encouraged by *someone specific*. Let me ask you something. What is going to change when they notice who you are? What is going to change when your dad tells you he loves you and he is really proud of you? What is going to change when they apologize? What is going to change when you finally get what you want? If there is a better version of yourself you envision becoming once you receive affirmation, then my next question for you is this: **Why wait?**

Why not just forgive them now and let it go? Why would you want to live your life with a backpack full of offenses?

ALLOWANCE

The best thing I have learned to do with offenses is this:

Let them go before they happen.

And this is why...

> **(NLT) Colossians 3:13** "**Make allowance** for each other's faults, and **forgive anyone who offends** you. Remember, the Lord **forgave you**, so you must forgive others."

I love the first two words.

Make allowance.

Give margin.
Provide leeway.
Leave a gap.
Create space.

The Bible is telling us to create a space in our life and in our world for other people to make mistakes. This means everyone in your life and in your world who offends you, *must* be let off the hook. Not should be. *MUST* be. Everyone. Leave some margin for the errors of other people in your life to make mistakes. While hurtful actions may offend you, don't let a one-time offense cause you a lifetime of pain. Let it go.

Let it go.

Let it go.

And move on with your life.

The worst thing you can do with an offense is pass it on. Hurt people hurt people. Offended people offend people. But you can be the one who drops the baton. It is a race you want to lose. I get it. Life was tough on you, which really means people made life tough on you. You may have hated it, but somehow you have become a conduit of it.

Maybe you experienced a difficult season so other people in your life wouldn't have to. Don't make other people pay today for what you were offended by 10 years ago.

There will be people who unintentionally offend us, and there will be people who deliberately try to hurt us. It's much easier to forgive a person who is apologetic toward you. It'll always be much more difficult to forgive a person who is planning on hurting you again. But Paul tells us to let it go regardless, because God did the same for us.

We must not forget we ourselves offend others all the time. Yet we tend to individualize offenses, as if we are the only victims of it. Not only are we not the only victims, we are the very ones who have committed the crime as well! Make allowance for other people's mistakes because you have them too.

(ESV) Romans 5:6 "For while we were still weak, at the right time Christ died for the ungodly. **7** For one will scarcely die for a righteous person—**though perhaps for a good person one would dare even to die— 8 but God shows his love for us in that** while we were still sinners, **Christ died for us.**"

When we were at our worst, Christ gave up his perfect life for our flawed ones. He has already made up His mind. He has not only forgiven our past mistakes, but our future ones as well.

Your greatest opportunity to be like Jesus is when you are being offended. If you could see the full picture of what the person who has offended you has been through, you would understand what they said to you has very little to do with you and a lot more to do with the brokenness they have experienced from somebody else. This is why we have to make allowance for each other's faults because if not, we only respond emotionally with a limited perspective on their life and ours.

LAUNDRY

Tuesdays are usually my longest workdays. Those are the days I get home pretty late, and by the end of it, my wife is equally exhausted from chasing around our toddler. There was one particular Tuesday I will never forget. My wife had washed the dishes and cleaned up the house during our son's naptime, but by the time I got home, our child had made a typical child's mess in our living room. They also ate dinner, so what had been clean dishes were now dirty.

Even though I had a really long day myself, I came home thinking it would be best for me to help out with the house and our child. I put in a couple loads of laundry, washed the dishes, and cleaned the living room. (Remember, I like to clean, but my wife likes to *deep* clean.)

After we put our son down for bed, I began folding our laundry and placed her folded clothes on her pillow on her side of the bed. This was an unspoken signal to her to simply play her part in doing the laundry by putting her freshly washed and folded clothes in their appropriate spaces.

As I was going back and forth between our bedroom and the laundry room, she called out, "Hey honey, I'm tired and not feeling well. I think I'm just going to go to bed."

I responded, "Ok, good night, sweetie." Then she turned off the lights and began to fall asleep. When I came into our room about 10 minutes later, I saw her folded clothes on

my side of the bed on my pillow!

I WAS LIVID!

My wife and I rarely argue out loud. We are both internal processors, so we argue with each other in our heads—but on the outside, we are super chill. But in this moment, I was standing in the dark about to flip our bed over with her in it. I can't recall a time when I was more angry in my entire life. I felt like a *butler.* I felt disrespected. I felt utterly... offended.

And then right before I was about to snap, she said, "Ryan..." I grudgingly responded with, "Yes?" She said, "Thanks for believing in me even when I don't believe in myself."

Come on, man. I can't stay mad at my wife after THAT statement. There was no way I could follow that statement with, "Well, I don't believe in you anymore until you put these clothes away." There was nothing I could say. Jesus momentarily calmed the raging seas in my mind with her sentiment. I decided to simply put the clothes to the side and made a plan to talk to her regarding how I felt about the laundry in the morning.

But then the morning came, and I simply swept how I felt under the rug. And if I am being honest, I held that offense against her without saying a word about it for two months. Every time I did laundry, I would find myself feeling bitterness toward her until one day, we pulled up the rug of our marriage and began to have healthy communication about the tension growing between us.

During this discussion, I began to tell her what I believed to be the root cause of why I was feeling offended at the time and I reminded her of that dark Tuesday night laundry situation. When I told her the story from my perspective, she started to giggle. I said, "What's so funny?" She said, "Ryan, I was pranking you. I was waiting for you to react but you never did. You thought I seriously would disrespect you like that? That's what you've been holding on to for two months?"

We laugh about it to this day because it was so silly. But what truly upsets me the most is that I allowed one offense on one night to turn into two months of growing bitterness toward my best friend. I swept it under the rug because somehow I thought it would be easier than dealing with it. Inevitably, my wife and I can talk more easily now about things we have been offended by because **we never want to leave room for a short-term offense to become a long-term separation between us.**

Address offenses early and often. Don't allow *one* unresolved offense to marinate in your relationships for months and years. The longer you leave an offense in limbo, the longer bitterness has time to grow in your heart. Attempting to have a functional relationship while dealing with *private* and growing contempt only leads you to having inauthentic connections.

Once again, the strategy of the enemy is to put distance between you and the people you love the most, one offense at a time. It is unreasonable to expect the people you love the most to apologize to you if they are unaware they have even offended you. Make a point to talk about offenses early and prepare to forgive others for them no matter what.

<u>JOIN THE PARTY</u>

The biggest err you can make in responding to offenses is by deciding the moment they happen how you are going to respond. Make up your mind right now that you are going to forgive people *before* they hurt you.

In fact, you can expect people will make mistakes that will eventually hurt you. However, making this decision does not mean offenses will no longer hurt. Remember, we are talking about being unoffendable—not invincible. We are talking about what to do with the pain, not pretending we don't bleed.

You're not Superman.
You're not Wonder Woman.
You will bleed.

But you don't have to keep opening the wound. **Being unoffendable doesn't mean you will never get offended, it means you choose not to *stay* offended.**

Jesus offered a parable that I believe helps us with this tension. He tells a story to give a picture of what the kingdom of God is like.

This is the story of the prodigal son. I'll recap the beginning of it, if you are unfamiliar.

Jesus tells a story about a man who had two sons and he divided his inheritance. The younger of the two brothers squandered his inheritance on what the Bible describes as "reckless living". He hit rock bottom and decided to come home. He thought his dad would be full of disappointment, but when he arrived, the father ran to him, kissed him, and began to throw a party for the son who had gone prodigal. When the party began, the Bible makes it crystal clear how the older brother felt about his younger brother's homecoming party:

(ESV) Luke 15:28 "But he was angry and refused to go in. His father came out and entreated him, **29** but he answered his father, 'Look, these many years I have served you, and I never disobeyed your command, yet you never gave me a young goat, that I might celebrate with my friends. **30** But when this son of yours came, who has devoured your property with prostitutes, you killed the fattened calf for him!' **31** And he said to him, 'Son, you are always with me, and **all that is mine is yours. 32** It was fitting to celebrate and be glad, for this your

brother was dead, and is alive; he was lost,
and is found.'"

While we are happy for the son who was lost
and became found, I think there will always
be a part of us that relates to the older
brother who just honestly wanted to be
celebrated himself. What the father tells him
in response to his resentment is, he could
have thrown a party anytime he wanted. Just
because people are not throwing the party
you want them to throw for you doesn't
mean you have any reason to refuse to
attend another person's party.

If somebody else gets more social media
attention than you, join the party.

If somebody else gets the compliment you
long for, join the party.

If somebody gets better, nicer, and newer
stuff than you do, join the party.

If somebody advances in their career, go to
the party.

If somebody finds a spouse before you, go
to the party.

And I don't mean, go to the party physically and be distant emotionally. It's possible to be somewhere and not be there at the same time. Really go to the party. When you refuse to celebrate other people in their achievements, you will begin to boil in phantom discouragement and become offended when you should be celebrating.

The older brother let phantom discouragement allow him to believe a good dad was a bad dad. Here's the deal. Whether you had a good dad, bad dad, or no dad... forgive him. Forgive the people in your life who have hurt you because not letting it go is only serving as a poison to your own destiny, not theirs.

Forgive them.
Forgive dad.
Forgive mom.
Forgive the teacher.
Forgive the ex boyfriend.
Forgive the ex girlfriend.
Forgive the ex spouse.
Forgive the current one.
Forgive your sibling.
Forgive your old boss.
Forgive your old friend.
Forgive the coach.

Forgive your last pastor.
Forgive the person who used a racial slur.
Forgive the police.
Forgive the government.
Forgive a President.

Let it go. Let it go. Let it go. Give all of the above the allowance of grace extended to your life by an Almighty God.

Please hear me when I say I am not excusing what anyone has done to you. I am truly sorry for every thing and every person who has ever hurt you. I am sorry for every person who never showed up for you. I am sorry for the racism you experienced. I am sorry for the sexual abuse. I am sorry for the verbal abuse. I am sorry they left. I am sorry they let you go. I am sorry they didn't choose you. I am sorry.

But can we invite God into this area? Will you give your pain to God? Your pain does not have to be a prison. Your pain has a purpose and managing it yourself can be exhausting.

I want you to allow God to free you from all the moments where no one encouraged you. I want you to allow God to free you from all the things that have been said to you, and all the things not said enough *to* you. Holding on to that offense, that pain, is robbing you of energy you could be using towards your future hopes and dreams.

One of the ways we become free from offense is by taking the initiative in becoming the type of person you want others to be for you. If you have been longing to be encouraged, noticed, and appreciated—then go find somebody who is discouraged, unnoticed, and unappreciated and be everything to them that you have always longed to have for yourself.

Choose to encourage others like crazy. Highlight the small, wonderful details about them. Appreciate what others bring to the table. There may be unresolved tension between you and someone you love all because you feel unnoticed, unappreciated, and undervalued by them. Stop allowing offense to put a wedge between you and those you love. Do your part. Notice them. Appreciate them. Value them. Whatever you do, don't live another day of your life stifled by the poison of offense. The story of the prodigal son is really a story of the *prodigal sons* because two brothers needed to know they could come home.

So I want to invite you back home. Home is the place where you can really be yourself without unrealistic expectations on other people. Maybe you have walked away from church because you experienced church hurt. I want to invite you to come back home, and to join the party.

Ultimately, to live an unoffendable life, you have to wrestle with a few questions:

What role have you allowed offenses to play in your life?

What unresolved tension have you allowed to destroy one of your closest relationships? Is there somebody in your life you need to forgive, but is there also somebody in your life you need to ask forgiveness from?

It's easy to feel as though the person who has hurt you owes you an apology. But can you imagine what your life would look like if you moved past your own pain and began apologizing for any pain you may have caused someone else? Can you imagine if you did that without comparing your pain to theirs?

When you can forgive offenders who are *not sorry* for what they did, and ask forgiveness from people you feel like you have barely hurt, then *offense will lose its grip on you.* The enemy wants to use offense to keep you bitter at the world, unhappy with your life, and distant from the people you care about. You cancel the enemy's plans when you allow forgiveness to govern your life.

Food for thought:

1. What does it look like for you to make allowance for other people's mistakes?

2. What does it look like for you to let go of past and present hurts?

3. Whose party do you need to go to?

4. Who do you need to forgive?

7

SMALL BALL

One of the perks of being a motivational speaker is I get the opportunity to meet all types of different people who have come from all around the world. One of the great things about being part of a larger church is you can literally meet a brand new person each week! It's fun. As I meet new people each and every week, the number one statement I get when I shake their hand is, "Man...You are a lot taller than you look on stage."

Apparently the lights, camera angles, height of the stage, and depth perception from their seat—whether it be in the balcony, far wings, or watching online—all add up to people believing I'm 5'7. Nope. I'm 6'3. Sometimes this is awkward because I am used to waking up to being tall every single day, but there are people who are legitimately shocked at my height when they meet me for the first time off the stage.

I had one lady come down to the front for prayer with tears in her eyes. My heart broke for her before she even said a word, and as she was wiping tears out of her eyes, she said, "You know, Ryan... dang, you tall." I was so tall she forgot what she needed prayer for.

Being tall has its pros and cons. Airplanes are not one of the pros. Airplane bathrooms are not made for me. Airplane seats are not made for me. Shopping for jeans is an emotionally and physically draining field trip. There is nothing worse than getting your hopes up when you grab jeans you think will be long enough, and then you hold them up to your waist, only to have the retail agent direct you to the "Big and Tall" section. The only problem with the Big and Tall section is I'm not Big and Tall... I'm just tall. I wear a size 12, not a size 18.

I will never forget the time my wife and I grabbed dinner with a friend of mine who recently passed away, Gail McWilliams. She was a dynamic motivational speaker and author who went to our church. Doctors told her she would go blind if she continued to have children, and she chose her children over her eyesight. She was a brilliant communicator who inspired people all over the world. Nevertheless, she was blind. I've known Gail and her husband, Tony, for years, and she asked me at dinner if I was working on any new, fun projects. I told her about the Chasing Failure project with the NBA. I gave her the scope of the project and how I was going to fail at the highest level.

She said, "So what's your thing you're going to 'fail' at?"

I responded, "Well, I'm going to tryout for an NBA team."

Gail was a conversationalist to the core. She never ran out of words. This was the one and only time I knew her where she went completely silent. And it wasn't the good kind of silent. It was the worried kind of silent where I could feel her thinking...

"Ryan... don't do this. As your friend, save yourself and me the embarrassment. Don't do this to us."

My wife leaned over to Gail and said, "Hey Gail, I'm not sure if you know this, but my husband is African-American, 6'3" and was an All-American basketball player in college."

Gail let out a huge sigh, "Oh, thank God."

You know, it was refreshing to sit with someone who could see beyond what most people see. She could only make calculations about who I was by what she could hear coming out of my mouth and heart. There are moments when people see me in basketball gear in public and say,

"Who do you play for?"

and I'll respond with,

"The Golden State Warriors."

Just kidding. I'll say, "Nobody", and then I'll have to briefly share my basketball story from college and why I pursued business and ministry instead of a professional basketball career. As I close the chapter of when I decided I did not want to spend my 20s playing basketball for a living, I can always see the disappointment on their face. It's as though they want my life to sound better. Have you ever had a moment in your life where you did not quite meet the expectations set for you by someone else? Maybe you thought it would just be easier if you could fit into the box they had created for you because then, at least you would no longer have to exert any extra energy explaining *why you are who you are*. There are moments where I think it would just be easier to be smaller.

Hugs would be a lot easier for me. Right now, most hugs are just awkward because most of the people in my life are less than six feet tall. Unless you get a running start, a hug with me is just not going to be successful. At least, by now, I have mastered the church side hug. Taking pictures would be a lot easier if I were smaller because I still have yet to figure out a way to hunch down in a position where it doesn't look like I'm hunching. My wife often says in pictures, "Ryan, just stand the right way." I'm trying! It's silly the amount of time I've spent trying to look right in somebody else's picture. I don't want to appear too tall or too short. What I want is to do the thing I think we all have the desire to do: *fit in*.

But neither you nor I were designed to fit in. We were designed to stand out.

SAFETY BOATS

I have learned while God has a plan for your life, so do other people. People have a picture in their mind of where they think you should be *by now*. You should have a house, a spouse, and kids *by now*. *You're still working there? You're still dating him*? People have a picture of what kind of car you should drive, what you should wear, how you should spend your money, and what you should do with your life. And anytime we go outside the lines of the picture frame they've set up for us, we have explaining to do.

I have watched far too many people decide to play small because someone said something that shook their confidence to the core. I have watched how one offense could keep a person from dreaming. I have witnessed how one offense could keep a person from believing in themselves altogether. It's no fun when you are keeping your biggest dreams a secret from your closest friends because we have all had relationships get weird from sharing too much information. It puts us in a vulnerable position to share our dreams. When we share our dreams, we actually put ourselves in a position to be offended more than when we just talk about the weather.

But in the event you grow tired of living inside the box the world has created for you to live in, the Bible has some encouragement for you. There is a man who, I believe, felt the pressure to play it safe as a follower of Jesus. This is a man who knew what it was like to face the timidity of standing out. He is also the only person in the history of the world to walk on water with Jesus; his name is Peter.

(ESV) Matthew 14:26 "But when the disciples saw him walking on the sea, they were terrified, and said, 'It is a ghost!' and they cried out in fear. **27** But immediately Jesus spoke to them, saying, 'Take heart; it is I. Do not be afraid.' **28** And Peter answered him, 'Lord, if it is you, **command me** to come to you on the water.'"

Peter's response to the fact that it was Jesus walking on water toward him is rather uncanny. Peter, if it was Jesus, then why play a game of truth or dare with Him? Why not just ask Him to calm the storm? Because that is what we would all rather have, right?

Stop the storm, Jesus.
Calm the pain, Jesus.
Command the waves to stop, Jesus.

Come on, Jesus, this is one of those moments to use one of your go-to moves. The winds and waves obey you.

We know that.
We can trust *that*.
There is safety in *that*.

The problem with *that* is... *that* was not enough for Peter. Peter was in search of something more that would challenge him. He was not only testing Jesus to see what Jesus could do, **Peter was curious as to what he was made of.**

And so are you.

(ESV) Matthew 14:29 "He said, 'Come.' So Peter got out of the boat and walked on the water and came to Jesus."

One of the most Googled questions of all time is, "Why am I here?" I have a feeling you might be reading this book right now with the same question, and you don't want to leave this planet never knowing why you were created to be here in the first place. But I also know you will never discover *who* you really are and *why* you really are until you step outside of your comfort zone.

Until you decide to position yourself into a place where you are no longer clinging to a life vest and a certain sense of safety, you will never find out what you are really made of. I believe every single person has a moment in their life where God calls them outside of their boat. I believe every single person has a moment in their life where God calls them outside of their comfort zone.

Perhaps you are reading this book right now, going through the greatest storm of your life, and you are just searching for a boat! You are searching for safe. You are searching for calm. Your life may appear to be put together on the outside, but if everyone could see what your life actually looks like behind-the-scenes, we would be engulfed by a constant, raging sea.

It's easy to make our lives appear to be more interesting on the Internet than the reality of our actual day-to-day experiences. It's easy for people to gather conclusions about our whole life from the highlights they see us post online.

We live in a society where a great job must equal a great life, a luxury car must equal financial bliss, and a soul mate must equal romantic euphoria. People think our family Christmas cards are a perfect depiction of how our families operate all year long. (We are always smiling and wearing matching outfits, right?)

We are deeply afraid of people finding out maybe we are unhappy when everything *they see* should add up to a happy life. But what the people who are paying attention to our lives, in person and on the Internet, can't see is the fact that none of the things we ever post about can bring true and lasting satisfaction to our souls. When we can feel the gap between our portrayed "*Internet us*" and the *real us*, we will always be tempted to make our real life look more like our Internet life. When we get around others, especially the ones who liked our most recent posts, we feel the temptation to do something God never wants us to do: *fake happiness*. Whether we realize it or not, there is a boat our world would love for us to stay in, and it's called the American Dream.

Can I be honest with you? (Thank you for giving me permission.) God's purpose and plan for your life is not for you to live the American Dream. God's purpose and plan for your life is for your faith to grow. The key ingredient you need for accomplishing your biggest dreams is not money, power, or fame. The key ingredient is faith, my friend.

You don't need your bank account to get bigger.

You don't need to be more connected to powerful people.

You don't need your social media following to grow.

You need your faith to grow.

In order to do that, you have to get past the

fears holding you back from your destiny, and choose to step out of the boat!

MORE THAN A FISHERMAN

One of the many things we know about Peter is that, although he was a devoted follower of Jesus in the story above, he previously would have experienced rejection just by the nature of his invitation to join Jesus as a disciple. We know this because of the nature of the Jewish educational system during this particular Biblical period. At this time, there were 3 levels of education for every Jewish male:

Level 1: Bet Sefer – House of the Book
Level 2: Bet Talmud – House of Learning
Level 3: Bet Midrash – House of Study

During Bet Sefer, 5 days a week, Jewish children were taught the Torah (the first 5 books of the Bible) in a local Synagogue beginning at the age of 6. By the time they were nearing 10 years old, they would've had **all of the Torah memorized**. Imagine having Genesis, Exodus, Leviticus, Numbers, and

Deuteronomy memorized. For most Jewish children, this was all the education they would ever need. Once they were finished with school, they would return home to learn the family trade (i.e. farming, carpentry, or fishing). In other words, they would learn to do whatever their family was known for doing.

The students who were considered to be the best of the best among the Jewish scholars were allowed to continue onto the second level of education, Bet Talmud. Here, they studied all of the Hebrew Scriptures, which would be equivalent to our Old Testament. And yes, you guessed it; they would memorize all of the Old Testament between the ages of 10-14. During this time, students also learned the Jewish art of questions and answers. Instead of answering a question with an answer, they were taught to answer a question with another question. In this way, students' knowledge and reverence for the Holy Scriptures could be tested. These young kids must have been extraordinary.

The 3rd level of education was Bet Midrash. The only way a student could even make it to this level was if they were knowledgeable enough to know the Scriptures as well as the back of their hand. The application process was brutal. Think Harvard law students. If a student was given the opportunity to go to a rabbi (teacher) to seek further education, the rabbi would grill the student and ask them all kinds of questions, trying to find out if they were good enough. The rabbi not only wanted to know if the student knew enough about the Scriptures, but more importantly, he wanted to know if that student could be like the rabbi in every area of their life.

Could he *talk* like him?
Could he *live* like him?
Could he *think* like him?

After vigorous testing, if the rabbi decided he didn't believe the student had what it would take to become a rabbi themselves, then the rabbi would tell the child to go back to the family business. *Go back to fishing.* Go back to making furniture.

In rare cases, if the rabbi thought highly enough of a pupil, he would extend an invitation to the student to continue being their teacher, and it would become their life's goal to become like the rabbi in every way. They would agree to take on his beliefs and his interpretations of the scriptures. This was called his "yoke" and he would say to the students, "Come, follow me." (When Jesus said His yoke was easy, He was essentially telling His followers that the way He interpreted scripture didn't place burdens on people like other rabbi's yokes.) Nevertheless, this was a huge privilege offered only to elite individuals.

At Peter's age, he had already been told to just go with the family business. He had already been told he was not good enough or smart enough to be anything more than a *fisherman*. That was, until Jesus showed up. You may have often wondered why Peter would immediately leave his job to follow Jesus. **It was because Jesus was offering Peter the opportunity to become who society had told him he could never be.**

Maybe you feel the same tension Peter did. Maybe you were rejected. Maybe you were not chosen for something, and that offense has shaped you. Maybe the thing that shakes your confidence is your family history. Maybe your dad went to jail, so expectations are low for you statistically. Dad slept around. Mom slept around. You might have generations of addictions to things that destroy lives, not build them.

But I believe you are reading this now to prove all those negative voices wrong. You are on the edge of the boat about to make a decision about your dreams, and today you have a shot at proving you're not a mistake. Maybe you're afraid that who you've been and what you've done may disqualify you from who you can become. So you play small and disqualify yourself before anyone else can.

Who told you that? Where did that come from, friend?

You are not here on accident. Regardless of what was said to you, or what maybe was never affirmed, God has orchestrated your life up to this very moment to let you know everything that has held you back was designed to set you up for greatness. There is something special about you that can change the world around you.

When I think about Peter taking his first baby steps onto that water, I can picture him telling himself... "I'm not just a *fisherman* anymore." **Don't let what you have been called in the past make you miss who you are called to be *today*.**

Peter's story concludes like this:

(ESV) Matthew 14:30 "But when he saw the wind, he was afraid, and beginning to sink he cried out, 'Lord, save me.' **31** Jesus immediately reached out his hand and took hold of him, saying to him, 'O you of little faith, why did you doubt?' **32** And **when they got into the boat**, the wind ceased. **33** And those in the boat worshiped him, saying, 'Truly you are the Son of God.'"

Yes, Peter almost drowned.
Yes, Jesus saved him.
Yes, Peter had his doubts.
Yes, Peter should not have had his eyes on the winds and waves and should have fixed his eyes on Jesus.
Yes, Peter should have had more faith and less doubt in his best friend.

But don't miss the best part of the story for Peter. Peter walked an unknown amount of feet to Jesus and almost drowned. And we know the storm did not cease until they both got back into the boat. So what we can conclude from this is... *Jesus and Peter walked back through the storm together.*

Peter got something in the deep water he could not get in the safety of the boat: **a walk to remember.**

Peter had every logical reason to play small, but where would his logic have gotten him? Where is it getting you? **Every offense you have ever experienced was designed to keep you in the boat**. Whatever you do, don't allow offenses to make you play small. My hope and prayer is that you would not allow past hurts to keep you from future dreams. My hope and prayer is that you would forgive the people who have offended you already, and the people in your future who inevitably will. My hope and prayer is that there would be a moment in your life where you and Jesus have a walk to remember. And no matter how bad the storm, I pray... you would never walk through any storm... without Jesus.

Food for Thought:

1. What's keeping you in the boat?

2. What would you do if you knew you couldn't fail?

3. What would you do if you didn't care what people thought about you?

4. When you are going through a storm, what or who do you lean on the most?

RECAP

In case you missed it, here are the 7 keys to living an unoffendable life.

1. Deal with the part of you that offends others. In everything you do and say, try to bring out the best in other people.

2. Live and measure your life by God's standard. Don't allow yourself to be offended when your life doesn't measure up to other people's expectations.

3. Love people that don't look like, talk like, think like, believe like, vote like, spend money like, or live like you.

4. Grow in the midst of being offended. Offense gives you an opportunity to grow your faith. On the other side of an offense is a blessing.

5. Invite honesty into your world. It removes the opportunity for offense to create space between you and the people you love the most.

6. Make allowance for people to offend you *before* they offend you. Forgive those who

have already offended you because holding on to the pain keeps you offended instead of allowing you to live in freedom.

7. Don't allow the fear of offense to keep you in your comfort zone. You weren't designed to fit in. You were designed to stand out.

One last verse, and we're done.

Proverbs 17:9 "Overlook an offense and bond a friendship; fasten on to a slight and—good-bye, friend!" (THE MESSAGE)

Don't lose quality relationships over small offenses. Let them go. Allow yourself to see beyond the offense and give the relationship the opportunity to heal. Being unoffendable is a choice. And when you make it, you give every relationship in your world a chance to thrive.

This last item is a gift for you. It's a new label. And it's one you should wear the rest of your life.